THE SCOOTER BOOK

By Bob Woods

HYLAS
PUBLISHING

THE
SCOOTER
BOOK

HYLAS
PUBLISHING

Hylas Publishing
Publisher: Sean Moore
Creative Director: Karen Prince

First published by
Hylas Publishing
129 Main Street
Irvington, New York 10533

Produced by
SHORELINE PUBLISHING GROUP LLC
Santa Barbara, California
President/Editorial Director: James Buckley, Jr.
Designed by Bill Madrid

First American Edition published in 2004
02 03 04 05 10 9 8 7 6 5 4 3 2 1

ISBN 1-59258-076-9 (WH)

Set in Caecilia and Base9

Printed and bound in England by Butler and Tanner Ltd.

Color origination by Radstock Reproductions Ltd, Midsomer Norton

Distributed by St. Martin's Press

Contents

6   Introduction

Just what is a scooter, anyway?

12   Scooter History

On the road to cool

24   Vespas and Lambrettas

The grand-daddies of them all

38   Scooter Culture

Movies, fashion, celebrities!

50   Buying a Scooter

Asking the right questions

62   The Scooter for You!

Classic, sport, or maxi?

84   Care and Feeding

Easy maintenance tips!

90   Scooter Travel Guide

Scooter-friendly U.S. and world cities

102   Scooter Clubs

Scooters fans gather for fun

112   Scooter Stuff

Accessories and gear

120   Glossary, Web Sites & More

126   Index

Scooter Mania!

You see them everywhere. From Abilene to Zebulon, Manhattan island to Manhattan Beach, Pike's Peak to Peekskill, they're all the rage. Hipsters ride them to cyber cafes. Baby Boomers add them to their "retro" collections. Urbanites commute to work on them. Coeds cavort around campus on them. Clubs members rally 'round them. And gas-station owners curse their fuel efficiency. They pop up in commercials, magazine ads, billboards, movies, and TV shows.

Save the earth: Ride a scooter

Scooters, once hip then out and hot once again…the coolest things on two wheels. Scooters are affordable, environmentally friendly, safe and easy to ride. They're cuter than a puppy when it comes to striking up conversations with total strangers. Scooters are a cinch to maintain. But mostly, scooters are a whole lotta fun.

The phenomenon dates back to 1946 and the creation in Italy of the Vespa, which remains the most familiar name in scooter-dom. With its barrel-shaped front, pot-bellied rear end, step-through frame, and single-cylinder engine, the Vespa became a universal icon. Along with the competing Italian Lambretta, introduced a year later, plus a slew of little-known, short-lived imitators, it spawned a transportation revolution that spread across Europe and eventually around the

Scooter stylin'

As the millennium turned, an old ride became a hot model again. Scooters, like this one on the Las Vegas strip, are "the" ride for the hip.

Fun ride

The 1950s (this French ad is from 1955) were the first heyday of U.S. scooter culture, as European style came stateside.

**Gregory Peck with Audrey
Hepburn in Roman Holiday**

globe. For example, congested cities in India and China, where space, parking, and gas are all at a premium, have long been scooter hotspots.

The scooter craze first hit America's shores in the 1950s. The 1953 movie *Roman Holiday*, with its romantic scenes of Gregory Peck and Audrey Hepburn buzzing around Rome on a Vespa, struck a chord and kick-started a fad. Vespas, Lambrettas, Toppers (the one and only scooter made by Harley-Davidson), American-made Cushmans, and Japanese models from Fuji and Honda enjoyed two decades of popularity in the U.S. However, more stringent emissions laws passed in the '80s stalled the market, leaving the scene to serious scooterists.

In Great Britain and other parts of Europe, the scooter culture continued, however. Scooters came to symbolize

Scooter cutie
Vespa put out annual calendars featuring scooters and models.

Early scooter style
While Vespa created its own look, other early scooters, like this 1950s Malaguti, looked to motorcycles for their inspiration.

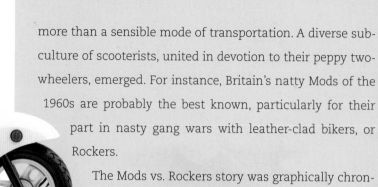

more than a sensible mode of transportation. A diverse sub-culture of scooterists, united in devotion to their peppy two-wheelers, emerged. For instance, Britain's natty Mods of the 1960s are probably the best known, particularly for their part in nasty gang wars with leather-clad bikers, or Rockers.

The Mods vs. Rockers story was graphically chron-icled in *Quadrophenia*, starring Sting, the music of The Who and a cavalcade of outrageously customized Vespas and Lambrettas.

Japan's version
Though Europe was the first source of scooters, Japanese mak-ers, such as Honda (above) entered the U.S. market, too.

Scooters conquer America—again!

In the late 1990s, scooters got caught up in America's retro trend of resurrecting things of cool past. Suddenly, long-for-gotten vintage bikes were hauled out from garages, barns and attics. Spit, polish, and spare parts brought them back to life. Lovingly restored scoots began drawing attention and reborn scooterists spread the word.

Among those who heard it, loud and clear, was Vespa, still a major player in the international scooter game. In 2000, the Italian legend burst back into the U.S. market with upgraded ver-sions of their classic designs and a network of groovy boutiques to sell them. Before you could say "Ciao, baby!" the likes of Jay Leno, Sandra Bullock, and Vin Diesel had joined the Vespa vogue.

A scooter under there
Decorating one's scooter has been part of scooter culture from the beginning. The addition of mirrors and chrome was pioneered by the British Mods.

8

The turn of the millennium also saw an influx of jazzy imports—echoing the look of racy, Euro-style motorcycles, only in a more civilized package—from Italy, France, Japan, India, Korea, China, and Taiwan that revved up a different breed of scooterists. They quickly embraced scooters as cheap, stylish alternatives to cars and motorcycles. Now they're riding them to work and play. And because humans have never been able to resist the urge to go fast and challenge each other, scooter racing has inevitably evolved into an action-packed sport.

As earlier generations did, American scooter riders today still look to Europe for style pointers. As we'll see, the accessories and fashion-world connections are a big part of the appeal for many urban riders.

Scooter fun

Easy to ride, two-passenger scooters can be a great way to see smaller, warmer cities. The 1952 ad below shows another use!

Meanwhile, the so-called "maxi" scooter—a sort of hybrid between a sport scooter and a touring motorcycle—with an engine up to 650cc has arrived on the scene. These sleek, high-performance, high-tech machines, from such makers as Honda, Yamaha, Suzuki, and Piaggio, feature models that can comfortably cruise at 90 mph.

The Scooter Book will cover 'em all. We'll identify top models and manufacturers, tell you what to look for—and what to avoid—when buying a scooter and accessories, plus steer you through some simple maintenance tips. Along with

Two for one
Some scooters can be equipped with sidecars, though it's recommended that dogs don't drive.

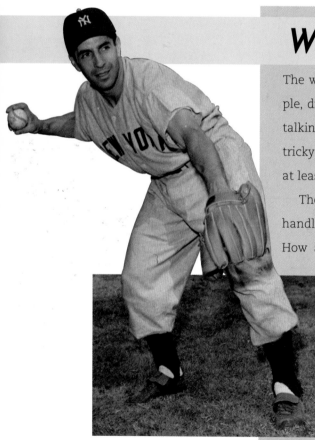

The Scooter

What the Heck is

The word "scooter" means different things to different people, dictionaries, and search engines. Here, of course, we're talking about motor scooters, though even that can be a tricky nomenclature. So let's start with what's not a scooter, at least in The Scooter Book.

Those two-wheeled skateboardy things with attached handlebars that kids push with their feet and steer? Not! How about the ones with little electric motors powering them? Not! The motorized, sit-down vehicles that senior citizens and folks with trouble walking ride? Not! One of those Segway stand-on contraptions? Not! The Hall of Fame shortstop for the New York Yankees, formally known as Phil Rizzuto? Not! (Okay, he is the Scooter, but you can't ride him.)

That brings us to the moped—and plenty of legal confusion, because every state has its own laws and regulations governing classification, registration, licensing, a time trip through scooter history (no tests will be given!) and a whimsical glimpse at scooter culture over the ages, we'll drop in on the scooter-friendliest U.S. cities and some of the hippest riding clubs, in the U.S. and around the world.

Scootering is here to stay as the hottest transportation option of the 21st century. Sales have grown by 500 percent since 1998, as motorcycle dealers, scooter-only shops, even lawn-and-garden centers fill the rising demand. And there's no end in sight. Scooters are the wave of the past, present, and future.

Scooter cutie II
Scooter makers are still very happy to have models posing with their latest, um, models.

cooter Anyway?

and insurance. Generally speaking, a moped is any two-wheeled vehicle with a bicycle-like frame, an engine under 50cc (cubic centimeters) or rated less than either two or five horsepower and that goes no faster than 30-35 mph. That's why you see tons of 49cc scooters, which often legally fall under the moped umbrella and don't have to be registered.

A scooter, then, has an engine over 50cc and hits higher speeds. Most states technically call that a motorcycle, though the engine has to be at least 200cc to take it on the highway. Either way, in most places, you need a special motorcycle license to operate it. As well, you may or may not need to wear a helmet.

The bafflement, unfortunately, is bound to continue. As scooters become more popular, states' laws are changing or being challenged. The best advice is to check with your state's motor vehicle department for up-to-date information.

Scooter cop
Italian authorities can track down your scooter on this Malaguti.

A Tale of Two

Early scooters
Italians perfected scooters, but French (above) and Danish makers were at work in prewar years.

Mention the word "scooter" and most folks immediately think Vespa. And rightly so. Cool looking, peppy, fun, and cheap, the quintessential scooter was a hit almost from the moment the first one rolled off the production line in Pontedera, Italy, in 1946. Arriving only a year later, the Lambretta, an equally stylish scoot made by Italian rival Innocenti, added to the excitement. Since then, Vespa parent company Piaggio has done a *magnifico* job keeping the brand name out front and its scooters updated. Lambretta, also much beloved among scooterists, mostly split the scene in the 1970s. (For more on both companies and their long rivalry, see the next chapter.)

However, a whole lotta scootin' went on long before Vespa hit the streets. In fact, the very first gas-powered two-wheeler produced in quantity dates to 1894 in Munich, Germany. Brothers Heinrich and Wilhelm Hildebrand, along with Alois Wolfmüller and Hans Geisenhof, created a machine dubbed the original *motorrad* (German for motorcycle). The Hildebrand & Wolfmüller, as it was formally called, featured a step-through bicycle frame supporting a

Wheelers

water-cooled, twin-cylinder, 1,489cc engine, a beast that produced a then-blazing speed of nearly 30 mph.

Aside from the step-through frame, it could be argued that the Hildebrand & Wolfmüller was more motorcycle than scooter, although technically the two terms are often interchangeable. Debatable nomenclature also clouds classification of the array of two-wheeled vehicles that appeared in the early part of the 20th century, as society shed its horse-and-buggy past and explored mechanized modes of transportation.

Simple stuff
Many of the earliest scooters, such as this bike-like version from 1920, did not boast the sleek styling and heavier frames of the scooters developed in Italy after World War II.

Getting started

In 1902, Frenchman Georges Gauthier introduced the Auto-Fauteuil, a jaunty four-stroker sporting a bicycle frame and a padded seat with armrests and a back. Denmark's Elleham followed three years later with a less elegant model. The initial U.S. entry, around 1915, was the Autoped, developed by the Autoped Co. of Long Island City, New York. This curious little machine looks remarkably like today's motorized stand-up scooter, right down to the fold-down steering column. Powered by an air-cooled, four-stroke, 155cc engine mounted over the front wheel, it came complete with a

Mods on a roll
Vast hordes of buzzing, bemirrored, parka-wearing "Mods" filled the streets of British cities big and small during the 1960s. Vespas and Lambrettas were their chosen transportation and a big part of their look and style.

headlight and tail-light, a Klaxon horn, and a toolbox. A British manufacturer, Norlow, came out with a similar vehicle at about the same time.

None of these were what you'd call big sellers, but a market, separate from that for motorcycles, definitely was emerging. By 1920, more than a dozen companies had joined the parade. Forty years before they gave us hipster Mods, the British treated scooterdom to the ABC Skootamota, the Kenilworth, the Mobile Pup, the Autoglider, and the Unibus. The latter two, preempting the Vespa, boasted full leg shields and storage compartments. France weighed in with the Monet-Goyon Velauto and Reynolds Runabout, while

Germany had the Krupp-Roller and Belgium the Moto-Car.

It's well worth noting that the vast majority of photos and ads for those early scoots pictured sophisticated women riding them. (They weren't predecessors of backseat biker chicks, either, although Vespa would make an art of illustrating and photographing lovely, leggy ladies for its annual pin-up calendars.) Remember, in many parts of the world back then women couldn't vote, own property, run a business, or even smoke a cigarette in public. One ration of liberation seems to have been scootering. Certainly the step-through frame allowed for wearing dresses and skirts, so it's possible that was the impetus for some designers. Regardless, scooters have from the beginning been marketed to and attracted women, to where today they account for at least half the ridership.

Ladies' day
With less power and simpler lines than motorcycles of the time, scooters quickly developed a following among female riders, such as this British adventuress on a French scooter from 1920.

New models follow the war

A handful of new brands of scooters roared onto the scene in the early 1920s. The British Jupp looked like a piece of avante garde geometric sculpture. The Ner-A-Car, the 1921 brainchild of American Carl Neracher, was an odd hybrid of an automobile, motorcycle and scooter. Produced simultaneously in the U.S. and England, it had a low center of gravity, giving it great handling, and a sideways-mounted motor that got up to 100 miles to the gallon.

In the midst of the Depression and a decade before the

American-made
Early American scooters included this (mostly unsuccessful) Nebraska-made Cushman Autoglide model.

Scooter racin'

Of course, as soon as Vespas hit the road, some guys started racing them. Short-track and long-course races are still held in the U.S. and European countries.

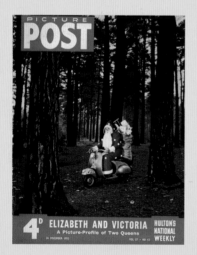

Scooter Santa

This 1952 magazine cover shows St. Nicholas buzzing through the forest on his handy-dandy Vespa.

Vespa buzzed to life, two significant scooters were born in America in 1936: the Salsbury Motor Glide and the Cushman Autoglide. The Motor Glide resulted from collaborative tinkering by Californians E. Foster Salsbury and Austin Elmore. The original wasn't much to look at—a lone rider sat atop what was essentially a tall rectangular metal box that housed a small four-stroke engine bolted to a running board and a pair of small tires—yet it succeeded by providing relatively clean, cheap transportation. Later models would be remarkably more stylish.

Meanwhile, Cushman Motor Works of Lincoln, Nebraska, pioneered a two-wheeled legend that would endure for nearly 30 years. A maker of engines primarily for farming equipment since 1901, the company decided to promote sales by hitching its sturdy two-stroke stars to scooters. The boxy Autoglide 1—usually called the "milk stool"—was released in 1936, and reportedly fewer than 20 were sold, but Cushman kept cranking out new models.

The Chicago-based Moto-Scoot Company put out a scooter in 1937 that was little more than a kid's push scooter with a half-horsepower engine. It sold well, and *Time Magazine* called creator Norman Siegal (rather extravagantly) "the Henry Ford of the scooter business."

Military models kickstart development

The fight for supremacy over World War II's European battlefields inspired several scooter manufacturers, on both the Allied and Axis sides, to develop military models. The most famous is the British-built Welbike, a no-frills, collapsible workhorse designed to fit into a metal cylinder, just 15 inches in diameter, and be parachuted from airplanes along with

paratroopers. The Welbike's proudest moment came on June 6, 1944—D-Day—as a number of them accompanied a group of brave men as they stormed the beaches of Normandy, France. After the war's end in 1945, surplus Welbikes were exported to the U.S. and sold in New York. By 1947, Britain's Brockhouse Engineering had retooled the Welbike into the Corgi scooter, which was marketed in the States by Indian, the revered motorcycle company as the "Papoose."

Cushman made a military scooter, too, the Model 53, employed by airborne troops stationed in Europe. (It's said that Enrico Piaggio based the MP5 prototype for his company's Vespa on military scooters he'd seen.) The Model 53 was retrofitted into a civilian scooter following WWII, with a spring suspension system and lights added. In the late 1940s and '50s, Cushman sold its scooters through Sears, Roebuck & Co. under the Allstate name. In 1961, the company signed

Stack 'em up

Lambretta was the major competitor for Vespa in the huge Italian scooter market. Here, this 1950s-era truck is loaded to the brim with new Lambrettas heading out from the factory.

Scooter from Sears?

That's right, you could order this fire-engine red Allstate scooter from the 1960s Sears catalog.

German scooter

This 1951 ad shows happy German folks enjoying rides on the "Goggo" model scooter.

a deal with Piaggio to import and co-market Vespas.

While World War II rid the world of Nazi terror, it left parts of Europe in shambles, physically, economically and emotionally. Scooters would play a role in the rebuilding efforts, getting factories up and running again and providing people with reliable and affordable transportation.

The atmosphere for innovation and creativity was fast and loose, not unlike during the 1990s dot-com boom. And just as that boom went bust, leaving the strong to survive, scores of scooter makers came and went before the better ones were left standing. Ironically, years later, a somewhat similar situation is occurring during the current scooter craze. Along with established names, newcomers are capitalizing. Inevitably, there will be a shakeout, and the survivors will take scooterists forward.

The rest of the world starts scootin'

Italian manufacturers Piaggio and Innocenti, with the post-war unveilings of the Vespa (1946) and Lambretta ('47), respectively, earned most of the attention, yet a slew of other companies' scooters were creating a buzz as well. Among other new-comers in 1946 were the Fuji (Japan) Rabbit, Gianca (Italy) Nibbio, Mitsubishi (Japan) Silver Pigeon, Powell (USA) Challenger and the Swallow (UK) Gadabout. By 1960, the burgeoning worldwide scooter land-scape included Bernardet (France), Iso (Italy), Moto Guzzi (Italy), Lutz (Germany), MV Agusta (Italy), Aermacchi (Italy), BMW (Germany), Walba (Germany), Motobécane (France), Ducati (Italy), Puch (Austria), Rumi (Italy), BSA (UK), Heinkel (Germany), Ariel (UK), Peugeot (France), Zündapp (Germany), Triumph (UK), Kawasaki (Japan), Honda (Japan), CZ (Czech Republic), Harley- Davidson (USA), Vjatka (USSR), HMW (Austria), WFM (Poland), and Yamaha (Japan).

The European scooter revolution spread to America in the 1950s. Domestic producers such as Salsbury, Rock-Ola, Powell, Crocker, and especially Cushman had made some noise, but when Vespa and Lambretta

Canine sidecar

This scooterist built a special dog-sized sidecar for his furry friend.

Vive la France

Peugeot was more famous for its automobiles, but this Model 55 scooter shows its entry into that big market.

Big Nose

This bulbous-nose-coned scooter came from the Pitty company of East Germany.

The Cub

The leading scooter in America during most of the postwar years was the handy-dandy Honda Cub, which has sold 35 million units worldwide. It is still produced for non-U.S. markets.

expanded its rivalry to the U.S., the decibel level went way up (see next chapter). The Honda Super Cub, Mitsubishi Silver Pigeon, and Harley Topper were part of the fanfare, too.

The Cub debuted in Japan in 1958. A year later, it became Honda's initial entry in the U.S. marketplace. With a 50cc four-stroke engine, three-speed automatic transmission, and lightweight step-through frame, it was the antithesis of the big, burly Harleys, Triumphs, BSAs, and other motorcycles that had become popular and a whole lot easier to handle. Plus, with a price tag of less than $300, it opened up an entirely new base of first-time riders. "It's not a big motorcycle, just a groovy little motorbike," sang the Hondelles in their 1964 hit, "Little Honda." Little did they—or anyone else, for that matter —realize just how groovy the Cub would become. With 35 million sold to date in 160 countries (it's the best-selling motor vehicle ever!), Cubs are now produced in

a dozen countries today. It helped make Honda a superpower in the automotive field.

Bouncing back

The Silver Pigeon was imported and marketed in the U.S. by the Rockford Scooter Co. of Rockford, Illinois, beginning in 1958. Over the next eight years, six different Rockford scooters were sold through independent dealers and at Montgomery Ward department stores. Ward later imported Lambrettas as well, selling them and Silver Pigeons under the Riverside brand name as the Miami, Nassau, and Waikiki. Harley's one and only scooter, the fiberglass-body Topper, sporting a 165cc engine (with a lawnmower-type pull cord) and automatic transmission, enjoyed moderate success from 1960-65.

Vespa dominated the U.S. market through the 1960s and '70s. Honda, Suzuki, and Yamaha, while building their motorcycle empires in the States, added several sporty scooters to the product mix during the 1980s. Honda featured the Elite and Aero. Suzuki had the Rascal and Shuttle. Yamaha's entries included the Yamahopper, Riva, and Zuma.

The picture changed dramatically in the mid-80s when the U.S. government passed tough new vehicle-emissions laws to which many scooters of the day—particularly those with two-stroke engines—didn't comply. Lambretta went out of business altogether, and Vespa pulled out of the U.S. in '85, leaving the American market mostly to the Japanese, although they were more interested in selling motorcycles.

Scootering hardly faded away, however. A diverse corps of stalwart scooterists kept the flame flickering by never abandoning their trusty rides. They formed brand-specific clubs,

Stalwart scooterists
Though not supported by major Italian manufacturers in the 1980s, determined scooter fans stuck with their bikes, importing parts and creating clubs of like-minded devotees.

Honda's hottest

Early models of the automatic Honda Elite 80 (shown here is a 2003 model) kept scootering alive in the 1980s after Italian makers departed the American market.

Style points

Ads from then (1959, above) and now (2003, right) continue to mesh scootering and hip styling.

gathered for rallies, swapped stories, and traded tips on scarce parts. With the rise of the Internet, scooterists found another uniting medium, as well as a nationwide e-marketplace for buying and selling vintage machines and a way to stay in touch with scooter fans worldwide.

Meanwhile, in much of the rest of the world, scootering had become a way of life. Italy remained a hotbed, where Piaggio, Malaguti, Benelli, Italjet, and Aprilia competed for business with a steady flow of new models. Licensing deals to make Vespas and Lambrettas in France, Germany, Britain, India, Spain, and other countries propagated the species, too. Automotive giants in China, Korea, and Taiwan have become an important manufacturing base for various brands.

Today's booming market

Then, in the late 1990s, a handful of companies reentered the American market, gambling that the growing appetite for vintage bikes might lead to new generation of scooterists. Slowly but surely, Derbi, Malaguti, Kymco, Bajaj, Aprilia, MZ, Italjet, and other foreign manufacturers started setting up U.S. networks. Asian off-brand scooters—often not meeting safety and emission standards—entered the country, too. Finally, in 2000, Vespa came back with new models, dealerships, and plenty of media attention, which further legitimized the Stateside rebirth.

Some manufacturers have seized on the "retro" thing and

Malaguti

Yesterday

The Italian

Ford and Chevy. Pepsi and Coke. Beatles and Stones. PC and Mac. Vespa and Lambretta?

Vespa debuts

This ad in 1946 announced the arrival of Piaggio's trend-setting, style-defining version of the scooter. Riding on wheels had come a long way since the walk-on bike in the background.

Yes, in the annals of fierce rivalries and undying loyalties, the world's two most famous brands of scooters hold separate reserved parking spaces. These utilitarian-turned-fashionable vehicles were created at almost the same time, in the same country, each seeking to fulfill the same post-war need for basic, cheap, and reliable transportation. Yet there were fundamental differences —in design and mechanics— that ultimately generated two distinct camps of customers. So while the respective parent companies, Piaggio and Innocenti, locked horns in a pitched battle for market share, faithful riders—the Vespisti and the Lambrettisti —developed a friendly competitiveness with one another, not to mention pride in the scoots they rode, as the curious two-wheeled subculture evolved around them.

Those wars raged in the 1940s, '50s, and '60s, when the two titans vied over the

Stallions

release of new and improved models. Passions ran deepest on their home turf in Italy during arguments over who had the better, faster, cooler scooter. The point turned moot after Lambretta ran out of gas and sold its production rights in 1972. Piaggio has remained a major force in the worldwide scooter business, not only under the iconic Vespa name, but also Piaggio, and two Italian acquisitions, Gilera and Beta. In the U.S., today's owners of vintage machines rhapsodize over the bygone days of Vespa vs. Lambretta, but rather than try and rekindle them are more apt to join forces as fellow riders on the classic range.

Mr. Scooter
By the time this 1962 photo was taken, Enrico Piaggio, posing with a fleet of Vespas, was the reigning king of the scooter world.

The family business

The Vespa story begins two centuries ago in Genoa, Italy. There, in 1884, Rinaldo Piaggio, the 20-year-old son of Enrico Piaggio, founded a company to design and build ornate interiors of luxury ships. By the turn of the century, Piaggio was also building railroad cars and locomotives, and in 1915 expanded into the fledgling aeronautics industry, producing aircraft engines and eventually entire airplanes. The factory in the Tuscany town of Pontedera joined the Axis military effort during World War II, which made it a target of Allied bombing attacks, and a shambles as a result.

Building Vespas
This 1950s-era Italian Vespa factory shows the familiar body shape riding the conveyor belt.

Vespa prototype

This 1945 Vespa prototype had very little in common with what it would become only a year later.

A style emerges

While the scooter itself had its familiar shape by 1948 (above), ads were already extolling the many uses of the handy vehicle.

Piaggio, now under the control of Rinaldo's son Enrico, rose from the rubble with the rest of post-war Italy. Recognizing the public's desire simply to get around town freely again, and analyzing reports from exiled managers praising scooters they'd examined (reportedly a Cushman and an Italian Velta), Enrico instructed his engineers to devise a sort of two-wheeled equivalent of the Volkswagen — an economical people's scooter.

The first sting of the Wasp

The initial Piaggio prototype, assembled in 1945, was officially called the MP5 but internally nicknamed Paperino, Italian for "Donald Duck." It looked more like an ugly duckling—featuring a bulky, full-body cowling—and indeed foul looks doomed the project. Its saving graces were the curved leg shield and twist-grip gear changer. Piaggio then summoned his top gun, renowned aeronautical designer and inventor Corradino D'Ascanio, to refine the idea.

D'Ascanio, ignoring traditional motorcycle design, leaned

Versatility...
VESPA . . . with side car . . . for taking the children to school . . . to parties or just a local turn for relaxation and fun.

Picnics...
VESPA . . . Yep . . . just grab a basket and m'lady rides pillion . . . or perhaps takes her turn. Driving to the favorite lake, mountain, or river picnic spot.

Shoppers...
VESPA for Shoppers! All over the world Vespa folks find they save time and trouble . . . going to market . . . parking there and getting back home tool Packages go "inside" the trunk . . . on top of the back seat.

Sports...
VESPA . . . To the links . . . the lakes . . . the lagoon . . . golfers . . . fishermen, hunters too . . . pack your gear . . . any time of year, and off you go where you want to go via your wonderful Multi-Duty VESPA.

instead on his background in aerodynamics. He utilized light-weight sheet metal to sculpt the first production model, the Vespa 98. Its unique monocoque, step-through frame was constructed as a single, stress-bearing unit to provide strength and riding comfort. Powered by a 98cc, single-cylinder, two-stroke engine, it rode on eight-inch wheels. The engine, gearbox, and rear wheel assembly pivoted to provide rear suspension. The result combined functionality with elegance.

The little engine's buzzing sound, plus its rear end's resemblance to an insect's abdomen, led Enrico Piaggio to dub his odd-looking machine the Vespa, Italian for "wasp." The rounded script logo—highlighted by a curvy V that mimicked the scooter's shape—was emblazoned on the upper-right corner of the leg shield. It soon became a symbol for one of the most successful vehicles of all time.

Tapping the market

Unsure of how the public would react, Piaggio only built 2,484 Vespas in 1946. Its design generated mixed reviews from the automotive press, though road tests were generally favorable. Wrote Italy's influential *Motociclismo* magazine on April 10, 1946: "It is a vehicle which, unlike the traditional motorcycle proper, is suitable for all social classes and for both sexes. Its structure does not require excessive physical effort to get on, and is very easy to keep balanced in slow-moving traffic...The front apron protects the legs from dust and rain...It is the ideal vehicle for short town trips for businessmen, men of the professions, doctors, etc., who may park it in a public place and present themselves for their

Starring Vespa

Since its debut in 1946, the Vespa has been used by directors in a wide variety of American and foreign films, among them the following:

- **Professor Nachtfalter**
- **La Dolce Vita**
- **The World of Suzie Wong**
- **The Happy Road**
- **An American in Paris**
- **L'Avventura**
- **Roman Holiday**
- **The Conversation**
- **American Graffiti**
- **Quadrophenia**
- **Absolute Beginners**
- **American Pie**
- **Austin Powers**
- **Of Love and Shadows**
- **The Talented Mr. Ripley**
- **The Wedding Planner**
- **Bounce**
- **Along Came Polly**

appointments looking as perfect as though they had just got out of a car."

Increasing demand and mass manufacturing bumped 1947 production numbers up to 10,535. Then Vespa and the whole notion of scootering got a boost of legitimacy that year with the arrival of a competitor, the Lambretta.

While the two scooters themselves were both similar and dissimilar, their names would become intertwined for decades.

Like Vespa, Lambretta's roots stretch back to an Italian industrial giant, Ferdinando Innocenti, though his company's specialty was steel piping and tubes, used in scaffolding and plumbing. Innocenti opened his factory in Rome in 1926, them moved it to Lambrate, a suburb of Milan situated on the Lambro River, in 1935. And like Piaggio, during World War II, Innocenti was conscripted by Mussolini to shift to military production (his metal tubes were ideal for bomb-making).

Baby Lambretta
Vespa had competition when the Lambretta entered the market in 1947 (a 1948 model is shown).

Working bikes
By the 1950s, scooters had entered the work force, as shown by this 1954 British policewoman.

Lambretta makes its mark

Fortunately, Allied bombs didn't devastate key facilities at Innocenti, which also joined the reconstruction efforts after the war. Almost eerily, as if he and Enrico Piaggio shared the same wavelength, Ferdinando Innocenti had spied scooters during the war and later dreamed of producing low-cost ones for the masses. Remarkably, he turned to an aeronautical engineer, Pier Luigi Torre, to bring his dream to life.

Unmistakeable silohuette
Today's Vespas pick up the classic form of the original Italian versions, down to the placement of the familiar logo.

The Lambretta A (or M, as it was originally known) debuted at the 1947 Paris Motor Show, followed by months of ubiquitous radio ads intended to create a buzz before the challenger to the Vespa went to market. It differed remarkably from Piaggio's invention. Borrowing on what Innocenti knew best, the Lambretta was erected upon a tubular frame, based on that of a conventional motorcycle. Going for practicality over style, it lacked a protective cowling and full faring, yet boasted a more powerful 125cc engine, which was

There's a scooter back there, too

From the beginning, Vespa matched the beauty of its bikes with beauty of another sort, as in this 1953 ad.

mounted in front of the rear wheel, plus an optional passenger's seat. Within a year, nearly 9,700 Lambrettas were made—and the race against Vespa was on. Before long, Lambretta and Vespa clubs were forming, members swearing allegiance to their scooter—and plain old swearing at riders of "that other one."

An unmistakable sign of the rivalry was Vespa's upgrade to a 125cc powertrain in 1948. Two years later, Lambretta offered an LC version including a full leg shield and side cowlings, a relatively simple move that dra-

Trick riders
Promoting Vespas at every stop, these trick riders toured from Piaggio factories.

Classic style
This 1953 ad from Lambretta appealed directly to women, who had quickly become a big part of the scooter market.

matically increased sales. In 18 months, 42,500 LCs were built, along with 87,500 stripped-down Model Cs. Still, Vespa already had 100,000 scoots out the door by the time the LC hit the streets.

Even as Vespa and Lambretta slugged it out, a rash of Italian imitators helped foster an ever-growing scooter market up and down "the boot" over the next decade. Such names as Nibbio, Furetto, Iso, Moto Guzzi, Alpino, Rumi, and Frisoni joined the fray. But they all followed the two leaders, both of which steadily expanded and upgraded their product lines throughout the period immediately following World War II..

Scooter zoomin'

In Italy, Vespa sponsored numerous competitions among riders who wanted speed and style.

More power!

Vespa raised the bar in 1955 with the 150 GS, a milestone then and still a highly coveted vintage scoot. Reacting to riders' calls for more power and speed, better handling and sportier looks, the GS had it all. The 150cc engine and four-speed transmission made it the fastest Vespa ever. Its braking power increased, and the tires went up to 10 inches. Cosmetically, the larger, rounder, more aerodynamic GS was a stunner: newly designed handlebars incorporating the headlight; a sleeker leg shield; metallic gray paint job; and a longer, comfier saddle seat.

Comin' to America

With Italy conquered, Piaggio brought the Vespa to the U.S., as shown in this 1964 ad.

Maybe your second car shouldn't be a car.

Don't laugh.

It makes a lot more sense to hop on a Vespa than it does to climb into a 4000-lb. automobile to go half a mile for a 4-oz. pack of cigarettes.

To begin with, a Vespa can be parked.

It'll give you between 125 and 150 miles to a gallon. Depending on how you drive. And using regular gas.

The Vespa is a reliable piece of machinery. Its engine has only three moving parts. There's not much that can break. (People have driven Vespas over 100,000 miles without major repairs.) And it's so simple to work on, a complete tune-up costs six dollars. It's air-cooled. There's no water, no anti-freeze.

The transmission is so well built that it's guaranteed for life.*

Vespa has unitized body construction. The whole thing is made from one piece. It's not bolted together. It can't rattle apart.

If you buy a Vespa your neighbors won't move out of the neighborhood. The Vespa is a motorscooter, not a motorcycle. There is no social stigma attached to driving one.

There are six Vespa models to choose from. You can buy one of them with the money you'd spend just to insure and fuel

the average second car for a year. And you can count on getting most of that money back should you ever decide to sell your Vespa. It won't depreciate nearly as fast as a car.

You may laugh at the Vespa today. But tomorrow when you're stuck in traffic and one scoots by, remember this.

The laugh is on you.

Vespa

Rally time

Dozens of scooter-loving Italians roar off in San Remo, Italy, during a 1964 scooter rally.

The next big step forward came in 1977 with the introduction of the PX series. Available in 125cc and 150cc sizes, the restyled PX retained the classic Vespa look and added a few modern touches, such as squared-off side cowls, turn-signal lights, and a boxier front and rear end. The PX generated rave critical reviews, not to mention outstanding sales results. It remains perhaps the overall favorite series among the die-hard Vespisti.

Taking the scooter to the world

Piaggio cranked out its one millionth Vespa in June 1956, a benchmark of its phenomenal success. From 1946 to 1965, the year Enrico Piaggio died, 3,350,000 Vespas were manufactured in Italy alone, one for every 50 inhabitants. Political and economic upheavals during the late 1970s and '80s, as well as increasing competition from aggressive Japanese manufacturers, cut into the market's growth. Nonetheless, the number of Vespas produced has since risen to more than 16 million.

Innocenti built an ardently loyal following for Lambretta, though the company could never quite match Piaggio's financial, marketing, and production muscle. Its sleek LD model, offered in a 125cc version beginning in 1952 and a 150cc version in '54, became a landmark and the most popular Lambretta ever. The Li series, launched in 1958, was Lambretta's most elegant. Powered by a more powerful engine, the Li featured more curvy

Duke on a Vespa

John Wayne was among the many international celebrities featured in annual Vespa calendars.

and cleaner lines. It was the basis for all future Lambretta models.

Almost from the beginning, neither Piaggio nor Innocenti was content dominating just the scene in Italy. They both started thinking globally. Aside from exporting scooters, both companies entered into licensing agreements that let foreign manufacturers produce vehicles in their own countries.

Vespa aligned with Germany's Hoffman Werke, just north of Düsseldorf, in 1950, a partnership that lasted until 1954 when Messerschmidtt took over. In 1951, licensees in Great Britain (Douglas of Bristol) and France (ACMA of Paris) began production. Moto Vespa of Madrid brought the buzz to Spain in 1953. Bajaj Auto unveiled its Vespa 150 GS to India's masses in 1961. Although the two companies parted ways in 1971, Bajaj continues to build a Vespa-like bike, helping India become the No. 1 scooter market in the universe..

The Lambretta name entered India's lexicon in 1965 when API (Auto Products of India) became a licensee, an association that ended in 1988. When Innocenti halted scooter production in 1971, it sold tooling and manufacturing rights to the Indian government, which commissioned SIL (Scooters India Ltd.) to make the machines. Innocenti entered Germany in 1950. Spain's Serveta rolled out its first Lambretta in 1954, a tradition that continued until 1989, and

Conquering India

This ad for Vespa appeared in India in 1965. Vespa licensed its design to Bajaj in India in 1961 and the crowded country soon became an enormous market for the handy vehicles. In 2003, Bajaj brought its Vespa knock-offs to America.

Current Celebrity Vespa Owners

- Kirstie Alley
- Marc Anthony
- Matthew Broderick
- Sandra Bullock
- Robert De Niro
- Andy Dick
- Vin Diesel
- Flea
- Anthony Kiedis
- Matt Lauer
- Kirsten Dunst
- Carrie Fisher
- Dennis Franz
- Jimmy Fallon
- Wayne Gretzky
- Marcia Gay Harden
- Alyson Hannigan
- Milla Jovovich
- Lenny Kravitz
- Jay Leno
- Bai Ling
- Jon Lovitz
- Sarah Jessica Parker
- Jerry Seinfeld
- David Spade
- Steven Spielberg
- Sylvester Stallone
- Sting

in turn Serveta exported its machines to Britain, the U.S., and other countries. Lambrettas were built in Argentina, Brazil, Chile, and Colombia to feed the South American appetite.

And, of course, let's not forget the good ol' US of A. After a couple of flirtations with scootering in the early 1900s and again in the late '30s, outside of Cushman and Salsbury, things remained pretty quiet until 1951. That's when Piaggio started selling an "American" Vespa called the Allstate Cruisaire at Sears stores. A 125cc model, modified for the U.S. market—for the first time, the headlight was moved from the mud guard to the handlebar, where it would remain on all successive models—sold for $325. And it could be delivered right to the owner's front door!

Making scooters cool in America

Marketed to teens and moms as a neat, European-made alternative to a second family car, it took a little while to catch on, but within four years, 20,000 Allstates were purring around. An optimistic Piaggio established the Vespa Distributing Corp. in New York and a network of distributors. The exclusive Sears venture morphed in 1962, when Piaggio teamed with Cushman to become its official U.S. partner.

Keeping up with the Piaggios, Innocenti also invaded the U.S. in 1951; they later sold their .Model A 125D for $350 in the U.S..

As in Europe, where Vespa and Lambretta advertising and promotions were everywhere, the scooter started to creep into American culture. The famous scenes in 1953's *Roman*

Jimmy Fallon

Holiday of Gregory Peck and Audrey Hepburn scooting around Rome on a Vespa struck a romantic chord. Game shows awarded scooters as prizes. Vespa and Lambretta clubs started popping up. Hollywood stars and starlets wanted to be photographed on a scooter.

In the early '60s, Honda began its heavy push into the U.S. market, and sales of conventional motorcycles generally gathered steam, leaving scooters behind. By the end of the decade, internal problems at Innocenti were brewing, culminating with its demise in 1972. Even as the American market plateaued, Vespa continued to bring in new models, including the PX. In fact, the PX 150E would be the last Vespa imported into the U.S., in 1985, after which tough new emissions laws forced a 15-year hiatus.

Vespa continued to nurture its brand elsewhere around the globe before returning to America in 2000 with its ET 50cc and 150cc models, as a scooter renaissance took hold and competitors marched in. With its parent's typical panache, the newly established Piaggio USA signed up dealers who set up cute, retro-ish boutiques in major metro areas, such as Seattle, New York, Miami, and Dallas. The growing market for vintage scooters—with, not surprisingly, Vespas and Lambrettas in highest demand—served to solidify Vespa's resurgence.

Late in 2003, Piaggio made its boldest move of late, introducing the Granturismo, featuring a robust four-stroke, liquid-cooled engine, in either 125cc or 200cc (churning out a mighty 20 horsepower that'll reach 70 mph!). The Granturismo comes with 12-inch wheels, dual disc brakes, and a price tag of roughly $5,000.

You've come a long way, bambino!

Modern classic
Old-world styling and modern technology have met in Vespa's 2003 Granturismo model.

Keeping Up
with the

Scooter art
This 1958 poster shows the early influence of the scooter on art.

So what is it that makes scooters so ultra cool? Is it the thrill of riding unfettered—hair flying, wind rushing—over hill and dale? Is it the look of the funky-colored two-wheelers dashing down the boulevard? Is it knowing that they're on the cutting edge of vehicular vogue? Is it that nostalgic pang to recapture a token of the past? Is it that romantic longing to finally be Audrey Hepburn (or her handsome suitor, Gregory Peck)?

It's all that, and has been, pretty much since the beginning of scooter mania more than a century ago (OK, so we had to wait till '53 and *Roman Holiday* to kindle the Hepburn-Peck spark!). When a 1902 Auto-Fauteuil tooled along Paris' Champs-Élysées, there were plenty of oohs and aahs and ooh-la-las. Brits later gaped at the Skootamota, Autoglider, and Unibus, which were mostly expensive toys for the rich and famous—especially highfalutin' women who could ride them in their long, fancy dresses.

By the late '30s, when Yanks were gawking

Teen scream!
1950s pop icons Sandra Dee and Bobby Darin hopped onto the back of a Vespa during scootering's first rave era.

Scooterists

at Cushmans, Salsburys, and Crockers, scooters had achieved a measure of trendiness Stateside. They popped up in advertisements for high-profile products and on covers of tony magazines. Then, once Vespa and Lambretta arrived, a veritable scooter craze rocked the world. The Vespa is, declared *The Times of London*, "the most brilliant vehicle the Italians have invented since the chariot."

Italy leads the way

Stylish Italian scooters were being put on the automotive design pedestal alongside such icons as the Ferrari and Lamborghini. In advertisements they became synonymous with *la dolce vita*, Italian for "the sweet life." They appeared in fancy store window displays and model runways as essentials of haute couture. Once they spread across Europe and then the Atlantic Ocean, the scooters was undeniably the "It" girl on wheels.

Scooter chic played well in Hollywood. By 1962, at least 60 films had starred a Vespa. The illustrated cover of John Steinbeck's 1957 fantasy novel, *The Short Reign of Pippin IV*, had featured the hero on a scooter. Celebrities such as John

Anachronism on wheels
Under all that makeup, the bushy beard, and the ragged B.C.-era clothes is movie star Anthony Quinn, made up as Barrabas for a movie in 1961 but riding a non-Biblical scooter.

Calendar girl
Raquel Welch was just one of many hot celebrities to appear on Vespa's annual calendars.

Wayne, Charlie Chaplin, Natalie Wood, Charlton Heston, Paul Newman, William Holden, Britt Ekland, and Henry Fonda were hounded by the paparazzi whenever astride a Vespa. The annual Vespa calendar—graced over the years by Vargas girls, Raquel Welch, Ursula Andress, Jayne Mansfield and countless other beauties—quickly gained major pin-up status.

Mods and Rockers

The cultural spotlight caught scooters head-on when they became the vehicle of choice of England's teenage Mods during the '60s. A British version of America's iconoclastic Beat generation, gangs of natty Mods distinguished themselves by wearing sportcoats and ties under hooded military parkas, grooving to Motown tunes and ripping around on Vespas and Lambrettas accessorized with custom windshields, lights, mirrors, crashbars, and horns. In keeping with youth Darwinism, they had their rivals, the roughneck Rockers, who wore jeans and black leather jackets, preferred the day's heavy metal and rode BSA, Norton, and Triumph motorcycles.

Naturally, Mods and Rockers clashed, ultimately in weekend brawls at seaside resorts such as Margate, Clacton, and Brighton. The most infamous fracas, at Brighton in May 1964, was a bloody fight that led to dozens of arrests and public

Two Italian icons
What could be more Italian than Gina Lollobrigida riding a Vespa?

A Scooter moment

Scooter culture was recreated in the movie Quadrophenia.

Fame on wheels
Beloved by paparazzi and Vespa's owners alike, stars such as (top to bottom) Paul Newman, Gregory Peck, and Jean Seberg (riding on the back) took to scooters.

hand wringing over the plight of lawless teens. The story was immortalized in the 1979 film *Quadrophenia*. A far cry from *Roman Holiday*, it left an equally indelible mark on scooterdom. Indeed, the Mod look and attitude, including the love of scoots, remains alive and well in Britain and the U.S. today.

Scooter club culture

America's scooter scene during the 1950s and '60s wasn't nearly as dramatic, yet the zippy machines definitely generated passion and loyalty, especially among the clean-cut collegiate types that Vespa, Lambretta, and other makers courted. Scooterists formed clubs, which remained the lifeline of the subculture between the 1970s, when the fad waned and new models stopped showing up, and today's active resurgence in putt-putt popularity. Die-hards kept their scooters

Need more evidence that scooters have become a darling of pop culture? Entertainment lion MGM has invited Vespa to help celebrate the 40th anniversary of the Pink Panther. The ubiquitous cool cat was first

Think Pink

spotted in the opening credits of MGM's 1964 Peter Sellers movie of the same name, and from there went on to become a feline phenomenon in film, TV, and licensing. In 2004, MGM is rolling out exclusively designed Vespas along with an array of high-end products as part of a huge promotion behind the 40th (www.pinkpanther.com). The Hollywood conglomerate commissioned hip LA artist Shag to lend his "swinger's life" style, evoking the women, cocktails, lounges, sports cars—and, of

up and running, occasionally gathering with their fellow enthusiasts to reminisce about the old days and dream of a wider reawakening.

The voices of these classic scooter devotees grew louder during the 1990s, particularly across the Internet. Scooterists flocked to chat rooms and bulletin boards to exchange riding tales and ask maintenance questions. Online auction Web sites created a borderless e-marketplace for parts, accessories, memorabilia, and vintage scooters themselves.

South Beach style
The color and retro feel of Miami Beach are perfect for scooters.

course, scooters—of the fun-loving 1950s and '60s, to a body of Pink Panther artwork. The Vespa dealer in Santa Monica has Shag-icized several ETs, which will be displayed at the MGM Grand Hotel in Las Vegas, the Virgin MegaStore in New York and other sites. "If someone wants to buy one of these types of Vespas, they'll be able to call the dealer and he will create it," says Trish Halamandaris of MGM's consumer products division, who, coincidentally, used to run a Vespa franchise in Utah. She reports that a new Pink Panther flick, with Steve Martin reprising Sellers' hilarious French Inspector Clouseau character, may well feature Vespas. MGM is also showcasing a couple of "Panthered" Vespas at its shimmering new HQ in Santa Monica.

Not only America
As this 2003 Japanese ad shows, the renewed scooter craze is not limited to the U.S. Vespa and Malaguti are among several companies expanding into this massive scooter market.

Star power

When he's not swinging through the Manhattan skyline, Spidey, in the person of Tobey Maguire, scoots around town in Spider-Man 2. Jude Law (below) reprises the classic 1960s movie Alfie, complete with vintage Vespa.

The Illustrated Scooter Girl

Scooter culture has inspired San Diego-based artist Chynna Clugston-Major to develop a series of Scooter Girl comic books. Publisher Oni Press describes the story as a black comedy. "Ashton is the cool guy in town. He rules the school, and all the hipster chicks want to be with him. But then one day he sees Margaret, a vision of loveliness on a Lambretta. Ashton makes his move, but Margaret summarily rejects him—a whole new experience for a guy this cool."

Might Margaret be based on the artist herself, who happens to zip around SoCal on a silver Lambretta Li 150

The widespread trend toward "retro" things that evoked cool designs from earlier generations has proven to be a perfect fit for scooters. A new age of hipsters—Mods of a sort—have appropriated scooters, predominantly vintage Vespas and Lambrettas, as their alternative mode of transport.

This grassroots movement hardly went unnoticed by scooter makers, who've maintained healthy markets in Europe and Asia, where the snazzy, powerful sport and maxi scooters have joined the classic breeds. By the late 1990s, a few companies started testing the U.S. waters, importing new models and setting up a limited number of dealerships. In the land of pop culture, a fresh star was emerging.

The year 2000 proved to be pivotal in America's rebirth of scooter mania. That's when Vespa parent Piaggio launched a

Special? "I really obsess over anything that's visually stunning, and that's one subculture that centers itself around being visually stunning," Clugston-Major told *The Washington Post* in describing scooterists and their style. "It's about the way you wear your hair, the way you do your makeup, the kind of clothes you wear, the size of your lapel.

"Generally, people don't seem to pay that much attention to their fashion or their surroundings. For these people [scooterists], it's an entire lifestyle."

second invasion. Using the vintage craze as a springboard, they introduced the ET4 and ET2 models, vastly improved replicas of the original designs. The classic look was the same, but minus the hassles of kickstarting, manual transmissions, and sometimes unreliable mechanics. They start with the touch of a button, run smoothly, shift gears automatically, and stop on a dime.

Vespa's return not only legitimized the marketplace for others to enter, but helped nurture a whole new type of scooterist. People who have never desired to ride any type of motorized two-wheeler find themselves attracted to scooters for their cuteness, coolness, and stinginess at the gas pump. They won't break the budget, are a cinch to learn how to ride, and require considerably less space and stress to

Scootin' comic
Actor and comedian Andy Dick is an enthusiastic scooter booster.

Scooter stylin'
Like cars, highly-decorated scooters are also seen on the road, like this airplane-inspired design.

Fashion scoots on

The Malaguti company teamed with several fashion companies to display their bikes alongside the latest casual styles.

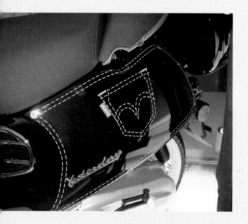

Blue jeans scooter

This Malaguti Yesterday features the familiar Levi's jeans stitching on the back cowl.

As with any passion worth its salt, or motor oil, scootering has spawned a magazine or two. In America, the "granddaddy," at the ripe old age of six, is *Scoot! Quarterly.*

Words of Whizdom

The 1998 brainchild of Barry Synoground and Casey Earls, a couple of intrepid San Francisco scooterists, *Scoot!* has been a lovingly produced, folksy, semi-slick conglomeration of news items, feature articles, often-hilarious accounts of local rides and rallies (complete with amateur snapshots), "Reader's Rides" profiles of awesome scooter projects, technical tips, and reviews of gear, accessories, music, and other lifestyle elements of interest.

Alas, as a labor of love in between real jobs, it just became too overwhelming for Barry and Casey, and in late 2003 they sold the quarterly 'zine to a Bay Area

park than a Suburban. There are affordable, reliable models to match every taste, whether it's Italian classic or motorcycle-ish racy. A 50cc scoot takes it slow and easy around town; 650cc maxis can cruise the highway comfortably at 70 mph.

While scooters proliferate from coast to coast, the nation's marketers—always on the lookout for the latest craze—definitely have scooters on their radar screens. They're "it" once again. Favoring "viral" campaigns over traditional advertising—where word of mouth (both online and off) can be incredibly effective and decidedly cheaper—scooter manufacturers' PR squads are soliciting the media to run stories, advertisers to showcase them alongside their

Bunny scooter
Playboy is one of several companies with branded scooters.

triumvirate of collaborators, Josh Rogers, April Whitney, and Mike Zorn. Editor Rogers—a veteran scooterist and owner of a 1962 Cushman, a Vespa 3-wheeler, and a Vespa Primavera—promised that it will remain faithfully fun, edgy and grassrootsy, but with "some changes in the focus of the magazine." While *Scoot!* has unabashedly catered to the vintage crowd, it will now serve up more coverage of new twist 'n go machines and those who ride 'em.

"We feel it's important to appeal to those people, too," concedes Rogers, who himself has just acquired a 2004 Vespa Granturismo. "We want to bring all scooterists together and make this the scooter magazine." The joys of scootering, he says, are "less about what you ride than your attitude about it."

Viva Georgio!
In Italy, actor George Clooney promoted a new scooter designed for medical emergencies.

The Futurist of Scootering

Watts Wacker is one of the few folks who can jot down "futurist" as his job title. In pondering trends that will shape the days ahead, the forward-thinking author, lec-

turer, political commentator, and social critic sees scooters as an increasingly important mode of transport. Indeed, he rides one himself, an aqua green Vespa ET4, to and from

products, movie studios to feature them in films and retailers to park them as catchy props in their stores.

Vespa has been especially aggressive. Try to find an article about the trend where Vespa isn't the highlight. Consider the products that have included them in ads and promotions, from Absolut vodka to Coke, Dell computers to Samsonite luggage, Pringles potato chips to Orbit chewing gum.

Vespa Barbie!
The American icon on an Italian icon.

the 19th century Victorian house that's home to his company, FirstMatter, in Westport, Connecticut.

A couple of years ago, after his minister challenged her congregation to "become more green," Wacker says, he sold his Camaro and downsized to a scooter.

"I used to be a car guy," he wrote in *The New York Times*. "I grew up in Detroit, where my dad was the advertising manager for Oldsmobile, and I owned a succession of big, powerful American cars. But the transition from muscle car to scooter has been incredibly liberating. I've gone from being macho to being Mr. Bean. In a way, the Vespa is the ultimate antihero statement: You have to be secure in your manhood to ride one. That's why I never considered getting a Harley—I would feel as if I were trying too hard."

Hotties on board

Women in general represent a big part of the scooter market. Celebs on the distaff side who sport scooters include Kirstie Alley (above) and Hilary Duff.

Starbucks gave away Vespas in a sweepstakes. Perhaps the surest sign of cultural inculcation, though, is the Barbie that comes with her own Vespa.

Just like in the '50s, celebs are lining up to be seen on scooters. Among its idols, Vespa counts Kirstie Alley, Matthew Broderick, Flea, Wayne Gretzky, Lenny Kravitz, Sarah Jessica Parker, Jerry Seinfeld, Sting and Ahmet Zappa. Scooters have starred in such recent movies as *Bounce*, *The Lizzie McGuire Movie*, *Chasing Liberty* and *Along Came Polly*.

Fads, of course, come and go. So there's no telling how long Hollywood and Madison Avenue will continue their infatuation with scooters. But as long as they're making scooterists feel ultra cool, it doesn't really matter.

Buying Tips

Finding the right scooter for you should be fun, not a complicated ordeal. There are basic considerations, but beyond that, it's pretty easy. Here are some useful tips to get you up and scooting.

What Kind of Scooterist Are You?

Choosing a scooter can largely depend on how you plan to use the thing. If you're just planning to buzz around town for fun on the weekends, a new or vintage model (see page 51) will do fine. You won't be putting on tons of miles or going too fast. So a 50cc scoot is all you'll need to reach speeds of 30-35 mph, even with a pal on the back. But if you want to ride it to and from work every day or do some serious traveling, definitely consider a new or late-model used machine—especially if you'll be taking it on the highway. On a 200cc scooter with 5 hp or more, you can com-

Scootin' around town?
Will you be using your scooter to do errands, as actress Gwyneth Paltrow does here in Beverly Hills?

fortably cruise at 55 mph and have enough juice to pass an 18-wheeler.

New or Vintage?

This is a serious consideration—and will ultimately say a lot about who you are and your approach to scootering. With a brand-new model, your choices are infinite. You'll have the comfort of modern conveniences, such as electric start, automatic transmission, and disc brakes. And a warranty can be a beautiful thing (of course, the longer the warranty lasts and the more it covers, the better).

When considering where to purchase a new scoot, it's wise to check out several different dealers. How long have they been in business? Is the shop clean and organized? Are the people running it friendly, knowledgeable, and helpful? Are they licensed by the state, or authorized to carry certain brands? What's their availability of parts, accessories, and service? Are the service people licensed and trained? Ask other scooterists for recommendations. You can usually check them out through the local Better Business Bureau or Chamber of Commerce.

A vintage scooter—typically more than 15 years old, but most date from the '50s through the '70s—can make a very cool statement about your hipness and turn lots of heads

Scootin' on the job?
Will you be using your scooter at work, as Swedish Formula 1 racer Kenny Brack does here in the garage area before a race?

(they're a better chick or guy magnet than a puppy, too). The vast majority are older Vespas and Lambrettas, though everything from a Cushman Highlander to a Heinkel Tourist can be found if you look hard enough. Because of the renewed interest in vintage scooters, lots of scooter shops offer both lovingly restored models and so-called projects, which come "as is" and require various degrees of work to get them on the road. Unless you're a fairly competent mechanic—or are willing to marry or hire one—steer away from a project scooter.

Even with a rebuilt vintage scoot, you should have some general mechanical know-how. It's a fact of life that older things require more TLC and break down more often, and if you can't fix 'em, frustration is apt to set in. Plus, how are you going to know that the machine you're buying is sound if you don't have some experience with engines, transmissions, brake systems, etc.?

Also, riding and basic maintenance are often more complicated with vintage scooters. Many have to be kick started and have manual transmissions (clutch and shift from gear to gear vs. an automatic twist and go). If your scooter has

Choosing vintage

Sure, a vintage scooter, like this mid-60s Vespa, is cool, hip, happening, and all that, but it comes complete with the idiosyncracies of a 40-year-old machine. Make sure you know what you're getting yourself into regarding care, parts, maintenance, and driving techniques.

one of the old two-stroke engines, you'll have to prepare a special mixture of oil and gas for fuel.

When buying a vintage scooter from a dealer, ask yourself (and the dealer) the same questions you would when buying a new one. Some will offer limited warranties. However, if you decide to buy a vintage or used scooter from a private owner, much more is more involved, especially if you do it over the Internet. As with a used car purchase, it's really a matter of trust and buyer beware. There are lots of vintage models on eBay and other auction sites, but are you OK with buying something like this sight-unseen?

Easy rider
Business uses for scooters include small delivery services, such as this fellow in Phoenix.

Liz goes shopping

Okay, Queen Elizabeth II didn't actually buy this Vespa, but scooters are certainly a permanent part of the British street scene.

Classic or Sport or Maxi?

Getting back to new scoots: Here again, what type of scooterist are you? If you're into retro, there are many different new and recent models designed in the classic Italian style. Start, naturally, with the real thing—a Vespa. Otherwise, Aprilia, Bajaj, Honda, Genuine, Yamaha, Malguti, Kymco, and others make Vespa lookalikes. Classics range in size from 50cc to 200cc and come in every color of the rainbow (and some that Mother Nature never dreamed of).

You don't need no stinkin' retro? You're the 21st-century, moderne type, who wants to be seen on a sleek, futuristic-looking sport model. There are endless choices, particularly in the smaller engine sizes. In fact, just about every manufacturer except Vespa

offers sport scoots (and Vespa parent Piaggio has you covered with its sport models).

Now, if you're in the market for a true highway cruiser that'll take you cross town or cross country, and don't want to mess with a manual-shifting motorcycle, go for the maxi. With engines from 400cc to 650cc, these babies fly. They shift automatically and have tons of storage room.

Goin' maxi

Maxi scooters provide more power, but at a higher cost.

How Much Can You Spend?

Ah, that nagging issue of money. You can spend a little or a bundle on a scooter. There are plenty of real cheapos out there, but we suggest you stay away from unknown brands sold on the side of the road. You can buy a new, brand-name scooter, with full warranty, for less than $1,000. Classic and sport models go up to about $5,000. A mondo maxi can set you back more than $8,000!

The price of a good late-model used scooter can vary. Vintage scoots are all over the place, too. A sweet Vespa or Lambretta from the 1950s can go for five grand or more. A do-it-yourself "project" scooter can be had for a few hundred. Do your homework, and shop around.

Gas isn't much of a financial consideration—a big reason for scootering in the first place!—but don't forget about all the riding gear and accessories you'll need to buy, along with license, registration and insurance, if required.

Classic style

This Vespa ET combines famous lines with modern technology.

Goin' shoppin'

Until recently, scooter fans had to brave the backrooms of motorcycle dealerships, but with the recent re-emergence of scooters in the U.S., full-service shops like this Malaguti outlet offer scooterists one-stop shopping.

Got Legal?

Every state has different laws regarding registration, insurance, safety equipment and licensing of scooters, which are generally classified as a motorcycle if the engine is larger than 50cc. As well, some states require riders and passengers to wear a helmet. (It's your body, but it's a smart idea to always wear a helmet anyway, along with protective eyewear and solid shoes or sneakers.) Your dealer should know the laws. For the official word, check with your state's department of motor vehicles; they all have Web sites.

Vespa comes back—big!

Piaggio's Vespa models can be found in big-city boutiques, such as this one in Denver, offering all the company's stylish models.

Gearhead Leno Scoots for Fun and Laughs

Riding a scooter "is fun," The Tonight Show host Jay Leno told *USA Today*. The late-night funnyman is well-known for his collection of classic cars, motorcycles and, now, three scooters. "It just makes you smile. People see you on it and they laugh, they smile, they beep and wave. Is it a fashion accessory? Sure. Is there some practicality to it? Yes." But is it as much of a babe magnet as his Lamborghinis and Harleys? "Women come up and go, 'What's that?' You explain it, then you have to explain that you're married."

Don't be scared off if you have to get a motorcycle license or need to learn how to ride a scooter. Choose a smaller, newer automatic model. You'll be amazed at how easy they are to handle. Consider taking a riding course offered nationwide through the Motorcycle Safety Foundation (www.msf-usa.org or call 800-466-9227).

Tips From a Pro

Bob Weindorf is a former motorcycle racer and lifelong motorbike fan. He started a scooter outlet in Santa Barbara, California, after having success importing and restoring vintage Vespas. In 2000, his shop became an official Vespa dealership when the company came back to America. He has some advice for those considering the new vs. vintage question:

A lot of people come in and love the look of the old bike, but those machines have their quirks. No matter how cool they are, they are old machines. They work just fine, but they don't have the conveniences of the new ones, mainly ease of starting.

The biggest thing for me, and I have both types [of scooters], is the vastly superior brakes in the newer models (as opposed to vintage). The old ones stop okay, but the new ones are just so much improved. Look at a 1960 scooter and a 2000 scooter...hey, that's 40 years of technology. They haven't just been sitting around putting out the same product.

With the new ones, you just hop on and go and get the enjoyment you were looking for. With the vintage ones, there's that level of additional care and work you have that might keep you off the road or reduce your initial enthusiasm.

Horning in

Scooters have become such classic style icons that even car manufacturers are using them to help sell automobiles, such as at this auto show, and in commercials.

Major Scooter Manufacturers

(American headquarter cities noted)

Aprilia USA

Woodstock, GA
www.aprilia.usa.com

Bajaj USA

South San Francisco
www.bajajusa.com

Beta (Eikon series)

N. Ferrisburg, VT
www.betamotor.com

Derbi Scooters

Miami
www.derbiusa.net

Genuine Scooter Co (The Stella)

Chicago
www.genuinescooters.com

Honda

Torrance, CA
www.honda.com

Kymco

Inman, SC
www.strmotorsports.com

Malalguti USA

Miami
www.malagutiusa.com

Peugeot

Cycle World Inc.
West Palm Beach, FL
www.mypeugeotscooter.com

Piaggio-Vespa -Gilera

Rancho Dominguez, CA
www.vespausa.com

Suzuki

Brea, CA
www.suzuki.com

Twist N Go (TN'G)

Preston, WA
www.tngscooters.com

Vespa USA/Piaggio USA

Rancho Dominquez, CA
www.vespausa.com

www.piaggiousa.com

Yamaha

Cypress CA
www.yamaha-motor.com

The Scooter

If you're in the market to buy a new scooter, there are dozens of different models to choose from these days. They break down into three basic design types: classic (or "retro"), sport, and maxi. In this chapter we're going to look at some of the best-sellers in each. Note: Not covered here are vintage scooters, the used or restored Vespas, Lambrettas, Cushmans, and other beauties from the past that are finding new homes. Check Chapter 4 for tips on what to consider before buying one of these legendary scoots.

Here's a quick rundown on each of the three main types of scooters:

Classic

Think Vespa. This is the quintessential scooter style: scooped front leg shield with a cute round light on top; rounded rear fenders surrounding the single-cylinder engine. Lambrettas of the 1950s and '60s featured a similar design, as did early models from Fuji, Honda, Yamaha, and Mitsubishi. Today's "retro" models from various international manufacturers appeal to scooterists who can't get enough of the classics.

For You

Sport

This is a pretty broad category that began in the 1980s when Honda and Yamaha departed from the classic look and went modern, with pointy snouts, sharper lines, and fiberglass moldings. As the latest U.S. scooter surge began in the late 1990s, the sport look went wild, emulating the racy Euro-look of "crotch-rocket" motorcycles. Nearly every scooter maker now offers a sport model.

Maxi

Short for "maximum," the name refers as much to the long, sporty look as to the larger engines that differentiate these ultra-modern machines. Consider the Suzuki Burgman 650cc, a space-age beast that looks more like a touring motorcycle, complete with disc brakes, adjustable shocks, and aluminum wheels. Its twin-cylinder, liquid-cooled powertrain will launch rider and passenger down the pike at 100 mph! Honda and Yamaha have comparable models, and the Piaggio X9 is expected to be introduced in the U.S. in 2004.

Vespa ET4

www.vespausa.com

The past, present, and future of scootering converge with today's ET4. The ET series was introduced by Piaggio in 1996, not only to celebrate the company's 50th anniversary in the scooter business, but also to symbolize its ongoing commitment to two-wheeling. While keeping the iconic Vespa design in place, the ET added modern touches, such as electric start, automatic transmission, a centrally mounted engine, and 10-inch wheels with front disc brakes. The ET2 ($3,000) features a 50cc, two-stroke, fuel-injected engine; the ET4 ($4,000) comes with a 150cc, four-stroke powertrain. Both are available in a variety of colors and with optional accessories.

Scooters

Bajaj Chetak

www.bajajusa.com

If this all-metal, a lot of a Vespa, of India contracted with lapsed, but Bajaj continues to monocoque-chassis scooter reminds you there's a very good reason. Bajaj Auto Ltd. Piaggio in 1961 to produce Vespas. The license make a virtual Vespa, and brought it to the U.S. in 2001. The Chetak is equipped with a peppy 145cc, four-stroke, nine-hp engine, a four-speed manual transmission, and electric and kick start. If you're looking for an old-style clutch-and-shift scoot with modern conveniences, at a price around $2,300, this is well worth considering.

Genuine Stella

www.genuinescooters.com

Like the Bajaj Chetak, Genuine's one and only model has a solid Vespa pedigree. Indeed, it's produced by another former Piaggio licensee in India, LML, for Chicago-based Genuine Scooters. Introduced in 2003, the all-metal Stella is basically a 1980s-style Vespa PX, at least in appearance. Beneath that, though, is a very 21st-century scooter. It's powered by a two-stroke, 150cc engine and a four-speed manual transmission. Attribute its comfortable ride to Bitubo gas shocks, a Grimeca front disc brake, and 10-inch Continental tires—all standard features at a starting price of $2,900. (Note: The Stella is not sold in California, whose stringent emissions standards don't allow for a road-going two-stroke over 50cc.) Available in red, mint green, silver, and tangerine, this classic scoot can be accessorized with such goodies as front and rear racks, cowl protectors, windshield, chrome hubcaps, and a striped mudflap. In its Fall 2003 review of the Stella, *Scoot! Quarterly* concluded: "For those who've never had the chance to own or ride a brand-new, classic-styled scooter, you're in for a treat."

Honda Metropolitan

www.powersports.honda.com/scooters

Strong evidence that scooters are here to stay in the U.S. is the growing number of Honda dealers that are opting to carry the two-wheelers, classic, sport, and maxi models. The classic Metropolitan ($1,750) comes with a four-stroke, liquid-cooled, 50cc engine, automatic transmission, electronic ignition, and plenty of storage space. It's offered in an assortment of two-tone colors, including Blue Hibiscus, Checkers, Kiwi, Sky, Denim, Salsa, Juice, Solar. An assuring safety feature is the combined braking system; apply the rear brake via the lever mounted on the left handlebar, and both the front and rear drums are activated. Among optional accessories are a rear rack or enclosed "trunk," windshield, and a basket that sits in front of the legshield.

As the name implies, this is a throwback to yesteryear's Vespas and Lambrettas, right down to the white-wall tires. Its fiberglass body includes modern adornments such as chrome trim and a faux spare tire cover that's actually a storage compartment. The Yesterday ($2,700) sports a 49cc, two-stroke, air-cooled powertrain, electronic ignition, automatic transmission, and a front disc brake.

Malaguti Yesterday

www.malagutiusa.com

Vespa Granturismo

www.vespausa.com

For the first time since 1996, Piaggio introduced a new model to the U.S. market in 2003. The all-metal Granturismo boasts a powerful four-stroke, liquid-cooled, 200cc engine, with a 20-hp maximum output, as well as 12-inch wheels and twin disc brakes. Available at Vespa boutiques throughout the U.S. for $4,900, the Granturismo is available in three colors—steel gray, black, and vintage green. Although this scoot's larger size prevents it from the convenient moped classification—which means you'll need a motorcycle license in many states—it satisfies those riders who want a little more oomph on city streets and the option of highway travel. Easily capable of maintaining a legal 65 mph, the Granturismo is a classic Vespa in a souped-up version.

TN'G Venice

www.tngscooters.com

Twist 'N Go's entry in the 50cc classic category has many of its own unique features that blend old-style design with state-of-the-art engineering. Between the cowls is an air-cooled two-stroke, which can be unrestricted to five hp, and an automatic transmission. The Venice's 10-inch wheels and extra-wide tires surround drum brakes. That's plenty of scooter for $1,595, but if you're looking for a little more zip but still want the classic look, TN'G offers the 125cc Milano for $2,195.

Yamaha Vino Classic

www.yamaha-motor.com

Chrome has long been a major turn-on for motorcy-clists, so why not brighten up a scooterist's ride with a bit of the shiny stuff? That's what sets the Vino Classic apart: a fully chromed front end—headlight, turn signal housings, speedometer, mirrors, handlebar, and steering stem—plus a chrome cargo rack on the back end. Adding power to the brilliant looks is a reliable 49cc, fan-cooled, two-stroke engine. Automatic transmission and electric start (and a back-up kickstarter) truly make it a get-up-and-go machine for $1,800. Its almost-identical twin, the Vino—minus only the chrome adornments—goes for $100 less.

Derbi Atlantis

www.derbiusa.net / www.cycleimports.com

Derbi, under the Piaggio corporate umbrella, offers a nice line of sport scoots. The lightweight Atlantis moves right along with its air-cooled 49cc powertrain and automatic tranny. No problem stopping, either, thanks to a front disc brake and rear drum. At $2,400, it's got plenty to offer.

Scooters

Honda Ruckus

www.honda.com

Honda has produced an unusual two-wheeled option with this cool little machine, almost a hybrid between a sport scooter and an ATV. With fatty tires and rugged, low-slung design, it's at home on the range and around town. The Ruckus is powered by a compact 49cc, four-stroke, liquid-cooled engine and an automatic, belt-driven transmission. Besides black and yellow, it's available in this camouflage color. It's a 10-pound scoot in a five-pound bag—for $1,900.

Kymco ZX50

www.kymcousa.com

The ZX50 is a high-quality, affordable sport scoot from the Taiwanese company that's swiftly making a name for itself in the U.S. market. It's ultra-modern looks are complimented by an efficient two-stroke, oil-injected, 49cc engine with automatic transmission, electric start, and front disc brakes. At $1,900 and with a two-year limited warranty, the ZX50 is a smart deal.

Malaguti F12 Phantom Digit

www.malagutiusa.com

You'll be coming of space age when you climb aboard this lightweight racer, known for its quick acceleration and tight handling, not to mention its streamlined Euro styling. At its heart is a high-performance, two-stroke, liquid-cooled 50cc engine. Dual disc brakes are included in this "Digit" model, along with a high-tech dash, featuring digital gauges. Blast off for around $2,350.

Piaggio LT50

www.piaggiousa.com

The sport counterpart to Vespa's ET2, the LT50 features motorcycle-ish 16-inch wheels, dual-arm front suspension, and a hydraulic front disc brake—making this 50cc, air-cooled scoot a snap to handle. At $2,200, the LT50 is a good choice for first-time scooterists.

The Del Rey—with a 125cc, air-cooled, four-stroke engine—provides that extra horsepower you need to make this a take-it-anywhere scooter. And it has the look that makes it welcome in any crowd, too. At $2,195, the Del Rey also includes dual rear shocks, a front disc brake, and plenty of storage space.

Vento Zip r3i TurboCam

www.vento-motorcycles.com

T his is a lot of scooter for around $1,300. It boasts a two-stroke, air-cooled, 49cc engine, hydraulic, sport-tuned suspension, front disc brake, 13-inch racing-type tires, aluminum wheels, a Silvertone exhaust system, a wireless remote-control ignition, digital clock, and an anti-theft security system.

Yamaha Zuma

www.yamaha-motor.com

You and the rubber of extra-wide, 10-inch tires will meet the road in sporty style aboard Yamaha's super-popular Zuma. You'll motor down that road pretty quickly and easily, too, thanks to a peppy 49cc, air-cooled, two-stroke engine and an automatic transmission. Sporty styling and bodywork create a racy package with an aggressive profile and riding position. They'll see ya comin', as well, with a headlight system that features dual bulbs with housings mounted on top of the faring. And with a bottom line of $1,700, you'll look even smarter.

Silver Wing ABS

www.honda.com

There are reports that a growing number of owners of Honda Gold Wing motorcycles are trading in their bikes for the company's Silver Wing maxi scooter. Both offer the ultimate in super-cruise-ability, only the Silver Wing offers it in an easier-to-operate design. There's just something about the step-through frame, automatic transmission, different wheelbase, and gads of built-in storage capacity that is bringing converts to the maxi style. The Silver Wing's powerful four-stroke, twin-cylinder, fuel-injected, 582cc engine is making friends, too. The latest models, offered in two-tone metallic silver/silver or candy dark red/silver colors, also feature an anti-lock brake system with discs, front and rear. It's a whole lotta vehicle for $8,100.

Scooters

Piaggio X9 Evolution

www.piaggiousa.com

The introduction of the X9 forefront of the fast-grow- hefty 460cc, single-cylinder, liquid- brakes, and a hydraulic front and rear end, the X9 provides superb handling and an incredibly comfortable ride. It looks pretty awesome, too. Evolution launches Piaggio into the ing maxi scooter market. Equipped with a cooled engine, an extra-wide rear tire, disc

Suzuki Burgman 650

www.suzuki.com

The Burgman 650 is turning heads, as well as opinions about scooters. This technological masterpiece brings the notion of "twist-and-go" to dizzying new heights. Twist, and this beast really goes, thanks to a powerful liquid-cooled, 638cc, eight-valve, twin-cylinder engine. The Burgman's unique transmission allows the rider to choose between a fully automatic mode or a manual shift mode. This maxi marvel comes with under-seat storage capable of holding two full-coverage helmets, plus three front compartments. The 650 version retails for around $7,900, while the Burgman 400cc, with many of the same features, goes for $5,600.

A Handy List of Scooters

Feel free to take THE SCOOTER BOOK to the scooter store when you go, but if you just want a handy list, here are all the models pictured in this chapter:

Maker	Model Name	Est. Price*
Classic		
Vespa	ET4	$4,000
Bajaj	Chetak	$2,300
Genuine	Stella	$2,900
Honda	Metropolitan	$1,750
Malaguti	Yesterday	$2,700
Vespa	Granturismo	$4,900
Twist 'n Go	Venice	$1,595
Yamaha	Vino Classic	$1,800
Sporty		
Derbi	Atlantis	$2,400
Honda	Ruckus	$1,900
Kymko	ZX50	$1,900
Malaguti	F12 Phantom Digit	$2,350
Piaggio	LT50	$2,200
Twist 'n Go	Del Rey	$2,195
Vento	Zip r31 TurboCam	$1,300
Yamaha	Zuma	$1,700
Maxi		
Honda	Silver Wing ABS	$8,100
Piaggio	X9 Evolution	$ TBA
Suzuki	Burgman 650	$5,600

*Not including tax, registration, accessories, and all of that other stuff.

Care and

You don't have to be a gearhead to own and operate a scooter...that is one of the beauties of the things. But you do need to keep an eye on things, as with any machine. Here are some maintenance tips that every scooterist can handle. No matter how much riding experience you have or how many scooters you've owned, step one is reviewing the handy-dandy owner's manual.

Adds Bob Weindorf of Vespa Santa Barbara, "Depending on the scooter, they might have regularly scheduled maintenance, but it's a big difference from a car, for instance, or even a larger motorcycle. It's just much easier, there's so much less to worry about."

So, while you keep on the regular maintenance with your local scooter pro, there are a few things you can do to keep your machine in good running order. As with a car or any machine, make sure it's cooled off before you start any work near the engine.

Feeding

Ready for takeoff
Modern scooters sport every type of gauge and dial needed to keep an eye on the bike. Some sport LED readouts along with traditional dials.

Before every scoot, check or test:

- Tire pressure, per your owner's manual or recommendations on the sidewalls of the tires. A simple pressure gauge works best. Many air pumps can be preset to shut off when the maximum pressure is reached. Also watch for excessive cracking and wear.
- Lights, turn signals, and horn.
- Brakes.
- Engine oil, fuel and battery levels. If your "dashboard" or instrument panel doesn't have alert lights, inspect manually.

Tire Pressure
Then and now, keeping your scooter's tires properly inflated is an easy way to make sure you get a good, safe ride.

Oil change

Most scooter dipsticks are easily accessible. On this Honda model, it's the little grey handle near the back wheel. Check your manual for the location of your own dipstick. The scooter's dipstick, that is.

Look Inside
The next pages give you a quick tour of scooters old and new

Every 1,000 miles

- Check brake and transmission fluid levels and replenish if necessary.

- If accessible. remove and inspect the spark plug(s) to ensure that the engine is running cleanly and efficiently. The lower part of the plug should be a golden brown with no oily wetness or carbon build-up.

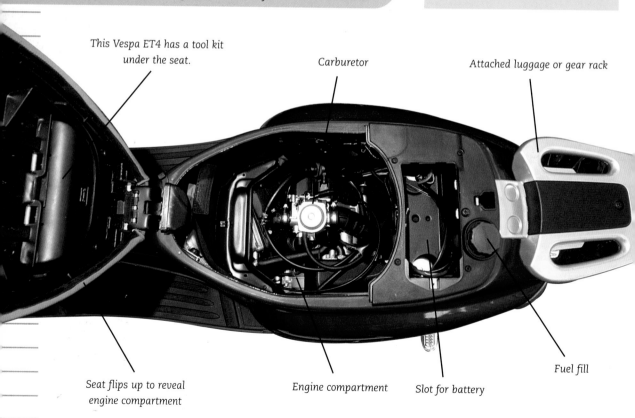

This Vespa ET4 has a tool kit under the seat.

Carburetor

Attached luggage or gear rack

Seat flips up to reveal engine compartment

Engine compartment

Slot for battery

Fuel fill

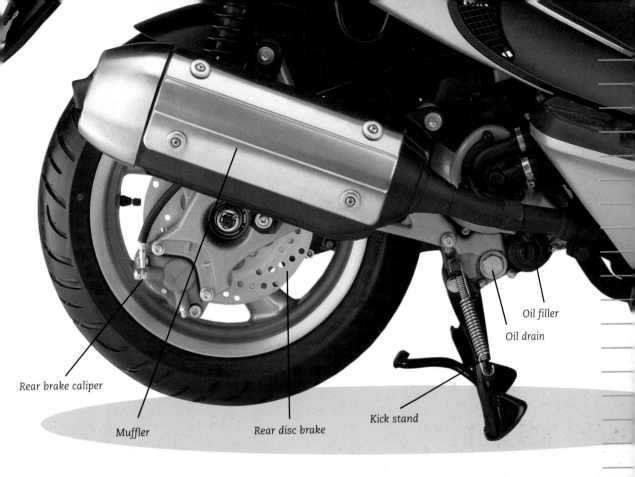

Rear brake caliper

Muffler

Rear disc brake

Kick stand

Oil filler

Oil drain

Every 3,000 miles

- Change engine oil and oil filter.
- Oil the throttle and brake levers and cables. Be sure they're properly connected and adjusted.
- Inspect the tension on the drive belt (or chain), per specs in the owner's manual. Avoid trying to adjust it as this can involve several tools and some serious time. If you feel that the tension is not up to specs, take the bike in to your dealer or repair shop.

Keep on scootin'

Vintage scooters need much more expert care.

Every 5,000 miles

- Change the transmission oil.
- Clean the air filter.

The old boys

Remember, these old bikes (this is a 1962 Vespa) have gears and a clutch like a motorcycle, so there is more skill involved—plus more parts.

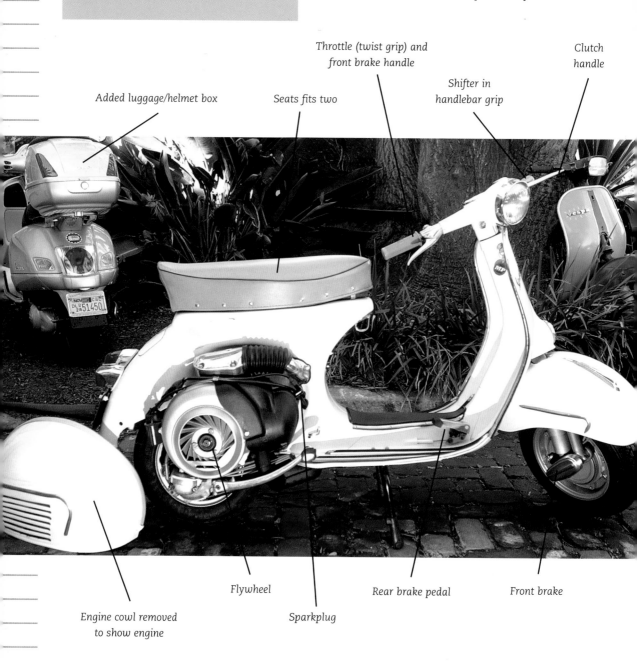

Throttle (twist grip) and front brake handle

Clutch handle

Shifter in handlebar grip

Added luggage/helmet box

Seats fits two

Flywheel

Sparkplug

Rear brake pedal

Front brake

Engine cowl removed to show engine

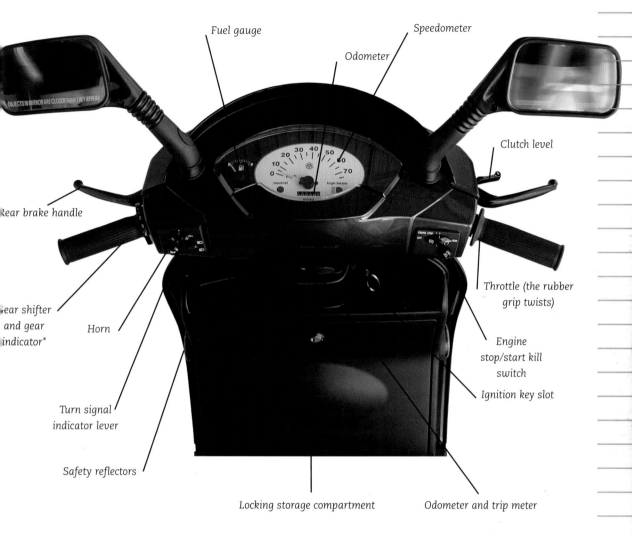

Fuel gauge

Speedometer

Odometer

Clutch level

Rear brake handle

Gear shifter and gear indicator*

Horn

Throttle (the rubber grip twists)

Engine stop/start kill switch

Ignition key slot

Turn signal indicator lever

Safety reflectors

Locking storage compartment

Odometer and trip meter

This shows a manual transmission Bajaj Legend instrument panel. Not every scooter control panel looks like this (automatics, for instance, don't have clutch and gears), and in fact some are much more sophisticated and high-tech, but it's a good look at what a typical scooter driver has at his or her fingertips.

In general:

- If you put your scooter up for the winter, charge the battery once a month.

- Keep a clean machine.

Travel

Few activities are more classically part of the scooter life than zipping through a bustling and/or beautiful tourist spot on a rented scooter. Through crowded streets or along quiet beachside lanes, along luxurious boulevards or beneath waving seaside palms, a scooter ride on vacation makes going home to your Toyota in the snow twice as hard.

Savvy American tourists, in fact, contributed to the recent re-emergence of scooters in the U.S. Upon returning from Italy or France or the Caribbean, they remembered their pleasant, parking-hassle-free rides on rental scooters and began to clamor for a chance to make the scooter life a permanent state instead of just a vacation idyll. American entrepreneurs then discovered that visitors to U.S. travel spots were looking for another way to get around town.

On the following pages, read about some of the most scooter-oriented spots in the U.S., plus discover a few ideas about destinations around the world where you can include scootering in your plans.

When traveling in the U.S., however, remember to check ahead about licensing requirements, which are devilishly different from state to state. It's not usually a problem in most foreign spots, however. So have a safe trip!

Scooter travel keys

Like scooter-friendly Key West (below), cities and towns that are mostly flat and boast good weather year-round tend to be great scooter destinations. When many attractions are located nearby each other, too, scooters are the perfect way to see the sights.

Scooter island

A pair of scooter riding tourists head to the harbor on Isles de Saints in the French West Indies.

Scooting in San Francisco

THANKS TO JONATHAN OGILVY, PRESIDENT OF SECRET SOCIETY SCOOTER CLUB FOR THIS REPORT: California, in general, is a scooter-friendly place thanks to year-round sunshine. This includes San Francisco, though the city's steep hills and narrow streets favor low-geared two-wheelers. When I was 15, it was the fact that, without a license, it was somehow less of an infraction to drive a scooter than to drive a car. By 16, I found myself braving every bridge in the Bay Area to attend scooter-related functions.

A few years ago I moved back from New York to find traffic and parking problems in San Francisco compounded. A few weeks after trading in my car for a Vespa Rally 200, I found myself among many old friends who had recently gotten their machines running again, as well as making new friends

Scootacular views
The end of a nice San Francisco ride means a view of the Bay.

who have found that this mode of transport takes people beyond their destinations. I'm not talking about falling asleep on the train. I'm talking awakened scootering—Transcendental Transportation, you might say.

Thus it makes perfect sense why, on any given day in San Francisco, you can spot a different scooter zooming in another direction. On special days, you can spot hundreds of scooters together. The Kings Classic three-day rally has been happening every August since 1993, and 18-year-old Scooter Rage is held in June. The first weekend in January is home to what Secret Society calls the Big Wet One.

The town is big enough to keep two friendly full-service shops specializing in vintage scoots in business (First Kick Scooters and San Francisco Scooter Centre), even with a host of freelance wrenchers lurking. There's also a Vespa boutique on Fillmore St. for the new models.

Weekly scooter jaunts take our crew of enlightened riders on a journeys through the deserted downtown, the crowded Embarcadero, or out to the golden countryside.

Mile High on Scooters

When Adam Baker and a partner opened Sportique Scooters in Denver in 1998, riders were few and far between. A handful of small shops and clubs around town catered to the vintage crowd, which included Adam. The notion to launch his own place came after he and a few fellow "scooter boys" made a pilgrimage to scooter-mad San Francisco. They hooked up with some die-hards, including Eric Halladay, proprietor of nationally known First Kick Scooters and co-founder of the Vespa Club of San Francisco. Adam went home inspired.

Today, Sportique operates three stores in the Denver area that carry new Aprilia, Kymco, Bajaj, and Genuine bikes, as well as rebuilt classics. Meanwhile, the Mile High City has become a scootering hotbed. "We now have thousands of new scooters in Denver. Even the motorcycle shops have stopped laughing and are selling scooters," Adam says. The first privately funded Vespa boutique opened here in 2000, too.

Denver is truly a scooter-friendly city. The majority of scoots are 50cc and under, thereby meeting the moped definition, meaning that you only need a standard drivers' license to ride one, plus a $5 sticker renewable every three years. It's even legal to park them on sidewalks and bicycle racks. Scooterists recently banded together to turn back a proposed state law that would have reclassified scooters with

(continued on opposite page)

New York Wakes Up to Scooters

Wen Schieffelin and her husband Zach, both native New Yorkers, opened a Vespa boutique in the Soho section of Manhattan in November 2002. Wen reports that the Big Apple is a ripe market for scooters, and is "gradually becoming a scooter-friendly city. Scooters are a fantastic alternative for a city with a lot of people in a dense environment," she asserts. "Just as in any large city, they make sense."

Scootering in NYC is not for the faint of heart, however. Whether you're in an 18-wheeler, a cab, a bicycle, a scooter, or even on foot, traffic rarely sleeps in that city, either, so you have to stay alert. A peppy two-wheeler does have advantages, though, like maneuvering through tight spots and sneaking into parking spaces not big enough for a Mini.

New York State law requires all scooters, regardless of size, to be registered and insured, and you need a motorcycle license and approved helmet to ride one (even to rent one). To the first timer, that might seem onerous, but Wen says not to worry. The Motorcycle Safety Foundation (www.msf-usa.org) conducts the equivalent of a driving school for motorcyclists and scooterists nationwide, including New York.

The Soho Vespa boutique sponsors various rides, club meetings (for both vintage

Biting the Big Apple
This trendy Vespa boutique opened in 2002 to help accelerate scooter growth in New York.

and modern riders). The annual Gotham Rally is a big scooter destination for out-of-towners on wheels. To get the scoop on various scooter clubs in the New York area, check out www.iscootny.com. Another source is New York City Scooterist magazine (www.nycscooterist.com).

More proof that New York is widening its scooter horizons is the news that Italian scooter maker Aprilia has also opened a dealership in Soho, on Spring Street, and reports are that Kymco may be setting up shop in NYC, too. Holy cow, as the Scooter (see page 10) himself might say.

(continued) wheels larger than 14 inches as motorcycles. This also makes the rental market a booming one.

The biggest annual Denver scooterfest, Mile High Mayhem, is held the last weekend of every July. Other big news is the addition of scooter racing at a go-cart track.

While riding around the city streets is standard fun, scooting out to the mountains is what makes the place so special. "From downtown, you can get there in about 30 minutes," says Adam.

Scooting's a Beach in South Florida

It's summertime and the livin' is easy year-round in Florida, where scooters are a common sight. Clubs and shops have sprung up and down the Sunshine State, along both coasts and in Orlando. Yet the beachy stretch from Fort Lauderdale, south to Miami and its trend-o-rific South Beach, and down to Key West is to scooters what Jimmy Buffett is to margaritas.

Tony Cappadona has owned a scooter shop in Lauderdale for nearly eight years, and he's witnessed the phenomenon first-hand. "It started in late 1996 when the only products were no-name Chinese models," he recalls. "One by one, Italjet, Derbi, Aprilia, and Vespa came in." Cappadona now

Head for the beach!

No visit to South Beach is complete without spotting zippy scooters filled with beautiful people.

runs a Vespa boutique, as well as a second showroom with Piaggio, Aprilia, and Kymco scoots. He's got a handful of pristine vintage machines, but concedes most of that business "to a few good shops that specialize in rebuilds.

"Folks ride scooters around here for transportation, as toys, and just for fun," says Cappadona, pointing to a smiling customer who just got a custom flame paint job on his black Vespa ET4. Cappadona has developed a specialty market, supplying scooters and the necessary rigging for deep-pocketed yacht owners who carry one or two on board. They come in handy when island hopping in the Bahamas, where cars are often scarce.

Joel Martin, president of Miami-based Malaguti USA, has been a part of Florida's scooter boom. It's a big market for the Italian company's 50cc scooters, which the state's DMV classifies as mopeds, so riders (and especially vacationing renters) don't need a motorcycle license. "Miami is creating a scooter social scene where there wasn't one," says Martin, who would like to see them become an everyday mode of urban transportation, "more of a necessity, as in South America and Taiwan." Hey, you gotta get to the beach somehow, right?

Scootering in Big D

In Dallas, they like to do things Texas-style. One scooter hangout is near a gnarly biker bar. "The older Harley guys really like scooters," says multiple-scooter owner Ron Bagley, with a modicum of surprise. "They remember having them when they were kids."

You won't see scoots and Hogs cruisin' side by side around Dallas, where scooters smaller than 200cc aren't even allowed on the highways. But that's OK, because there are plenty of wide open spaces and country roads ideal for scooters. Bagley and friends head out to White Rock Lake. "It's a casual, slow ride," he says.

Luis Rapini, who manages the Vespa Dallas boutique that opened in 2001 in the hip West Village development uptown, says scooters are beginning to fit into the super-size Texas culture. He sells about 20 new Vespas a month, many as "one more toy to have," but Luis sees the day when scooters will become a way of transportation in Dallas (below). It may not be like Italy, where he lived for five years, "but the scene keeps growing."

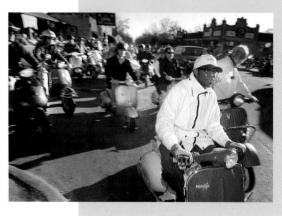

It's a Scooter World

America has been busy sending its culture around the world for decades, but in the world of scooters, the culture travels the other way. Today's celebrity riders and fashion-conscious trendoids are yesterday's Italian businessmen, British university students, and Chinese families. Scooters are an intrinsic part of many cultures around the world, as much a part of city life as traffic jams.

Travelers heading to various cities around the world can look to scooters as an alternative to battling subway crowds, a way off of the traditional tour bus, and a perfect opportunity to get up close and personal with the natives. Plus, of course, they're really cool. Here's a brief look at some scooter-friendly cities around the world.

Asia on the move

Many Asian countries are jam-packed with scooters, as in this street scene from Vietnam. The tight spaces and low cost of the scooters makes them ideal. Confident travelers can try scooters in many Asian cities, too.

(Another scooter hotbed is Italy; a scene from Siena is pictured at right.)

Viva Italia

Almost nowhere is more scooter-happy than beautiful Rome. From the Colosseum (above) to the Spanish Steps, scooters fill the streets at all hours of the day and night. Riding one is a great way to see the sights and blend in with the busy and colorful local culture.

ROME

Scooters can be found for rent in many places in the Eternal City. Kids as young as 16 can rent the smaller moped models. You can rent for a day or all week. Some tips: Stay out of the yellow-lined areas on streets, which are for public transport only. Keep off the sidewalks, especially around the popular Trevi Fountain area. You need a valid U.S. or International drivers' license plus your passport to hop on a scooter and hit the Roman road.

LONDON

Scooters have been racing around London since the years before World War II. The 1960s Mods brought them to a new height of publicity. In 2000, a nationwide fuel shortage brought the scooters back into prominence, though they had never really gone away.

Visitors can rent scooters by the day or week with a U.S. or International license. Remember, they drive on the other side of the road over there, so be careful!

PARIS

City of romance...city of traffic. Scooters can be rented as in most major cities. Motorcycles are more popular on Parisian streets than other European cities, so be prepared to do a little bit of battling. However, away from the busy boulevards, scooters make for a perfect way to discover that out-of-the-way restaurant or nightspot. Plus, of course, you look *tres chic*!

Outside of Europe, hot scooter-friendly places include Bermuda, most smaller Caribbean islands, and the busy streets of large Asian cities. Have fun!

Other Hot Spots
- **Southern Spain:** The coast of the Mediterranean sprouts scooters like sangria. British and French vacationers spend hours buzzing around on rentals.
- **Bermuda:** Few cars and lovely roads make for a scooter paradise.
- **India:** Massive numbers of scooters jam the busy streets; no shortage of repair shops!
- **Taiwan:** Especially in busy Taipei, scooters are everywhere.

Paris on wheels
Whether off to work or on the way to a quiet tete-a-tete at a sidewalk cafe, scooters are a great way to see the City of Lights.

Scooter Clubs

Scooter clubs can range from a couple of people to a couple hundred members, all of whom can range from hearty partiers or long-distance cruisers

"I refuse to join any club that would have me as a member."
— Groucho Marx

Those well-worn words from Mr. Marx might well apply to the scores of scooter clubs multiplying around the country like bugs on a smiley rider's teeth. Beyond a common affection for two-wheelers and step-through frames, some clubs' members delve pretty deep into debauchery. Just visit their Web sites and read the blogs—and hope there's a lot of designated driving going on.

Still, it's the love of scoots that brings all types of folks together to ogle each other's machines, compare mechanical notes, swap tales about tracking down rare parts, and ride, ride, ride. Most clubs are relatively small, with 10-20 members, and big cities generally spawn several different clubs. Vespa and Lambretta clubs, not surprisingly, are the most popular, though others are brand-specific, too. Most clubs meet monthly or even weekly and gather every weekend to ride, usually on Sundays (weather permitting, in the wintry climes, of course).

There are organized, national clubs, like Vespa Club of America and Lambretta Club USA. Others, such as Jedi Knights and Secret Servix, have chapters in more than one city. Vintage owners have been at it for a while, and some of their clubs remain exclusive to classic scooters. More and more, though, welcome anyone, regardless if they ride an old or new scooter.

The following list represents a sampling of various scooter clubs around the country. Some are well-established, others fairly loose, so don't be surprised to find less-than-active ones here. With new ones organizing all the time, scooter shops are great sources of information for potential club members. Shops also the perfect place to recruit members if you want to start your own club, too. Scoot! Quarterly magazine also has listings in each issue.

Mixed marriage?

Some clubs stick to one brand of scooter; others welcome both riders of both vintage and modern bikes.

Arizona

Pharaohs SC*, Phoenix

Founded in 1997, this branch of the club founded in San Diego meets the first Saturday and the third Sunday of every month and has an annual rally. Branches also in Texas, Michigan, Utah, and San Francisco. Contact: arizona@pharaohssc.com at www.pharaohssc.com

California

Sneaky Devils SC, Sacramento

This all-girls club meets every Tuesday night at the Rubicon Brewery in mid-town Sacramento. Contact: marion@sneakydevils.com; www.sneakydevils.com

The Vespa Club of San Francisco

Affiliated with the Northern California Scooter Council (NCSC). "We take it pretty easy, buy what we need when we need it and get together once a week." Contact: vcsf@vespa.org; www.vespa.org/vcsf.htm

Secret Society SC, San Diego, San Francisco

Considered the longest-running classic scooter club in the U.S., sponsors numerous rides and rallies, including Scooter Rage. Contact: SF - ogilvy2@earth-link.net; SD - drdubrow@netzero.net // http://secret-society.org

First and Last Chance SC, East Bay Area (Oakland/Berkeley)

Just a bunch of local people who want to ride. Contact: colby14@hotmail.com // www.flcsc.com

East Bay Wrecking Crew, Oakland

Member mostly ride Lambrettas, but some Vespas, too, and new members are always welcome. Contact: todd@sunrace.com

*SC stands for "Scooter Club," of course!

Showing off

A big part of every scooter club meeting is checking out everyone's latest scooter upgrade or accessory.

Vespa Club Los Gatos

Founded in 1989. Meets the first Sunday of each month at noon in front of the Los Gatos Coffee Roasting Co. downtown. Sponsors annual Classico Moto Italia rally in May. Contact: vespaclublosgatos@yahoo.com; www.vespaclublosgatos.com

Santa Cruz Vampires Motorcycle & Scooter Club

"Our purpose is to promote motor biking and scootering for our own amusement. Ride whatever you own". Contact: vampires@tower.org; www.santacruzvampires.com

Push Start Motor SC, San Luis Obispo

Classic scooter club meets first Sunday of every month downtown at Fosters Freeze at noon. Contact: lambretta@thegrid.net

Unforgiven SC, Bakersfield

Central Valley classic scooter club sponsors the annual Hedonism Rally. Contact: unforgivensc@hotmail.com

Vespa Club of Santa Barbara

Meet every Monday at 6 p.m. at the historic Santa Barbara Mission. Contact: info@motoparadiso.com; www.vesparados.com

West Side SC, Santa Monica

"No politics, no dues, just scootin'!" Meets for rides first Sunday of every month at 1 p.m. at Tommy's. Contact: westsidescootrclub@hotmail.com; www.vespaape.com/wssc

South Bay SC, Torrance

All scooters and/or two-wheeled vehicles are welcome. Weekly Wednesday night rides at 7 p.m.

Monthly rides every Saturday at 12:30 p.m. Meet at Claim Jumper's Restaurant. Contact: mario@3d-advertising.com; www.avia-art.com/southbaysc.html

Colorado

DCD(Denver City Denver) SC

"A loose conglomeration of local scooterists," as one member describes it. Claim to fame is the annual Mile High Mayhem rally. Contact: PamScoots@aol.com; www.milehighmayhem.com

Bottle Rocket SC, Denver

"We're a club for people who have classic metal-bodied scooters by any manufacturer," but anyone's welcome at rides and meetings, held every other Wednesday at Pint's Pub at 7:30 p.m. Contact: bottlerocket@brsc.org; www.brsc.org

Secret Service SC, Denver

"Our club is full of strong brilliant women who ride vintage scooters." Founded in Denver, with branches in New York, Florida, Georgia, Portland, and California. Contact: missi@lambrettagirl.com; www.lambrettagirl.com/ServixGirls.html

Killer Bees SC, Fort Collins

Welcomes classics, moderns, metals, and plastics, the only requirement being that members enjoy scooters. Contact: www.killer-bees.org

District of Columbia

DC Vintage SC

Vintage scooterists get together about twice a month at various locales around DC to discuss, fix and ride. Contact: tpsteele@mindspring.com

Florida

High Endurance SC, Orlando

"Dedicated to the riding, restoration and customization of classic scooters." Hosts annual rally during Bike Week near Daytona Beach. Contact: www.highendurancesc.com

Tampa Two Stroke SC

Loosely organized club whose members ride Vespas, Lambrettas and "a few odd-ball scooters here and there." Meets on weekends to ride and work on scoots. Contact: kieranwalsh@mindspring.com; www.tampatwostroke.com

Lambretta Club USA

The Lambretta Club USA is a national organization for Lambretta motor scooter enthusiasts. We support members in their efforts to document and preserve Lambretta history, as well as to enjoy Lambrettas through riding and competition. As a club, we are always looking for ways to promote Lambrettas and work with retailers to see that parts and service remain available here in the United States.

The club was founded in March 2003 and is recognized by the European Lambretta Club Council in July 2003. Members are located throughout the United States, as well as ex-pats and servicemen overseas. Current membership is about 100. The first U.S. National Lambretta Jamboree will be held in Miami, January 28-30, 2005.

Membership benefits include access to International Lambretta Club functions, a club tool exchange with all of the tools needed to keep your Lambretta on the road, discounts at Lambretta parts retailers, discounts on Lambretta appraisals, a club newsletter, LCUSA patch, and membership card and the opportunity to meet and enjoy the company of fellow Lambrettisti.

There are numerous national Lambretta clubs around the world that could be mentioned, but the two that standout are the Lambretta Clubs of Great Britain and Italy. Both maintain excellent Web sites and provide a wealth of information.   —Jay Fichialos (quadmod@scootourist.com), president

The Vespa Club of America

VCOA is a non-profit organization dedicated to collecting, restoring, and preserving European motor scooters. Since approximately 70 percent of them sold in the U.S. were Vespas, most members are Vespisti. However, many prefer Lambrettas. Some favor other models, such as Heinkels or Zundapp Bellas. Despite its emphasis on Vespa, the VCOA welcomes anyone interested in European marques. The VCOA publishes the American Scooterist magazine, hosts the annual Amerivespa rally and promotes scootering in general in the U.S. Contact: vcoa_prez@yahoo.com; www.vespaclubusa.org

Amerivespa 2004

VCOA is pleased to announce Amerivespa 2004 in Salt Lake City, Utah, June 24-26. Amerivespa 2004 will be the 12th national scooter rally sponsored by the Vespa Club of America. Amerivespa rallies feature rides, show n' shine contests, and many more activities.

Vulcan SC, Ft. Lauderdale/Miami

Hosts annual Hurricane Run from Miami to Key West. Meets at King's Head Pub, Dania. Contact: lammy125@aol.com; http://membres.lycos.fr/vulcansc1/florida.html

Georgia

Fist City SC, Atlanta

"An informal, mostly unorganized club dedicated to riding Lambretta, Vespa and other vintage scooters." Contact: deck@fistcity.org; www.fistcity.org

Imperial SC, Atlanta

"Members own vintage and new, two- and four-stroke, twist 'n go and shifter scooters." Meets Wednesdays at 7:30 p.m. at Thinking Man Tavern. Contact: contact@imperialsc.com; www.imperialsc.com

Illinois

Los Corazones Negros, Chicago

For motorcycles and scooters painted black. Meets every Monday night at Carol's Pub. Contact: bandit@burtreynolds.org; www.burtreynolds.org

Second to Last SC, Chicago

Meets first Wednesday of every month. Contact: benign@flash.net; www.22lsc.org

Jedi Knights SC, Chicago

Branch of the well-known classic scooter club. Contact: xwing@rcnchicago.com

Indiana

The Agents SC, Indianapolis

Meet every other Wednesday evening at Moe & Johnny's. Contact: jeff@180design.com; www.180design.com/agents

Louisiana

Jedi Knights SC, New Orleans

The Degobah chapter scoots in and around the Big Easy. Contact: nola@jksc.org

Maryland

Baltimore Bombshells SC

"Founded for women in and around Baltimore to meet, ride, and share information. We're not scooter snobs. Your choice of scooter is your business." Contact: BaltimoreBombshellsSC@yahoo.com; http://baltimorebombshells.actiongirlart.com

Massachusetts

Boston Stranglers SC

"Some of Boston's best hardcore vintage riders in town, we are the wilder side of the scooter scene." Meets every Sunday for dinner at the Common Ground in Lower Allston around 7:30ish. Also hosts

Second to No Scooter City

"Chicago has got to be the best city in the country for scooterists." So declares Chad Schaefer, leader of Los Corazones Negros, a scooter and motorcycle club in the Windy City. "Well, the best city that gets snow," he clarifies, looking out his frosted window in early February. "The streets are always plowed and salted within a few hours of the first snowflake, and that makes for year-round riding—as long as you bundle up."

As for things riders do, bundled or otherwise, Chad reports that Chicago has several active scooter clubs. "Of course, there's us, and Second to Last, 2Slow2Go, So1o, and the Jedi Knights."

The No. 1 scooterist hangout in Chicago is Club Foot, claims Chad, who started riding six years ago, first on a Yamaha Riva 200 and now aboard a 1981 Vespa P200. "The drinks are cheap, the rock and roll is loud and eclectic, and on weekends you can see members of almost every scooter club in Chi-Town, as well as Euro and Japanese vintage bikes."

Los Corazones Negros meets every Monday night at Carol's Pub, which Chad describes as "a genuine hillbilly bar with a selection of country music on the jukebox that's better than anywhere I have seen." On Thursdays at Neo, you can spot Vespas and old Honda motorcycles lined up outside and groove to real '80s alternative music inside. "There are tons more places and things to do," Chad says. One of his faves is riding Lower Wacker Drive in a pack of scooters, "like a swarm of angry bees in a tin can. "there's nothing like that in the world."

During the warmer months, Los Corazones Negros hosts weekly rides and random activities "to keep all the scooterists active and bring us all together," Chad says. "Chicago is not only my home, it's the home for scooterists."

Chicago is also home to Philip McCaleb, one of the pioneers of the current scooter scene. He started Scooterworks USA, Inc. in his basement in 1989, with the idea of cataloging and selling vintage Vespa scooter parts and accessories. Since then, "we've taken it to another level with catalogs and distribution that allows people access to materials to repair and restore their old scooters," Philip says. He wasn't satisfied with promulgating just the old stuff, though. Under the name Genuine Scooter Co., he and a former Piaggio executive joined forces with LML of India (formerly a Piaggio joint venture) to build new copies of the old and much-revered Vespa PX series. Thus, the Stella was born.

Scooter Racing: Full Throttle

The competitive desire to go faster than the other guy or gal is as primordial as our innate needs to eat and sleep. Hey, why do you think they call it the Human Race? And although scooters have this rather benign personality among their automotive brethren of greater displacement and horsepower, it's only natural that the "mine can beat yours" mentality would kick in sooner or later. Thus scooter racing maintains a place in the sports pantheon.

Piaggio, Innocenti, and other post-war European scooter makers battled it out early on as a way to gain a publicity and engineering edge over one another. By the mid-50s, France was hosting a 24-hour endurance race. The current Isle of Man Scooter Rally has attracted enthusiasts for nearly as long. Even NASCAR has staged dirt-track scooter races in years past.

Today in Europe, scooters are regularly included among classes in motorcycle races. The British Scooter Sport Organisation, for one, runs events for all makes and sizes of scooters, classic and automatic, solo and with sidecar. In the U.S., the sport is building traction, with several fledgling groups sanctioning races.

The American Scooter Racing Association (http://scooterracing.info) holds a half dozen events—five in California, one in Las Vegas—for vintage and modern scooters. The circuit draws up to 40 competitors. Mid-America Scooter Sports (http://www.whizwheels.com/mass.html) sanctions events in the Midwest, while the Eastern Scooter Racing Association (http://groups.yahoo.com/group/ESRA) is attempting to set up an East Coast circuit. Visit www.whizwheels.com for news and updates.

New England's largest scooter rally, on Cape Cod, every summer. Contact: woody900@attbi.com; www.bostonstranglers.com

Minnesota

The Regulars SC, Minneapolis-St. Paul

"A club for vintage scooterists in the Twin Cities area. Our goal is to gather often, enjoy good health and ride in mass as the gods intended." Meets at uptown Pizza Luce on the first and third Sunday of each month at 2:00 p.m., weather permitting. Contact: www.minnescoota.com

Minnesota Maxi SC, Minneapolis-St. Paul

Better known as Minn-Max, primarily for maxi scooters, though they welcome all scooter riders. Rides second Saturday and fourth Sunday of the month, mid-April through mid-September. Contact: MinnMax@maxiscooters.org; http://autos.groups.yahoo.com/group/Minn-Max

Missouri

Upsetters SC, Kansas City

All-inclusive club meets every Sunday afternoon at Scooter Fix/El Torreon. Contact: info@upsetters.net; groups.yahoo.com/group/upsetterssc

New Hampshire

New Hampshire SC, Manchester

"Scoot Free or Die." Informal group tries to ride whenever they can. In the meantime, they maintain a great Web site. Contact: www.nh-scooters.com

New Jersey

Sole Runners SC, Northern NJ

Close-knit group of Lambretta enthusiasts spanning the tri-state area.
Contact: http://solerunners.warmattic.com

New York

Checkered Demons SC, New York City

Vintage scooterists. Contact: checkereddemons@hotmail.com

Sunday Riders, New York City

Meets every Sunday at 1st Ave. and Avenue A in the East Village at 1 p.m., ride at 2. "Everyone welcome! Unless it's storming, we're riding." Contact: www.iscootny.com

Hornets SC, Long Island

"We scoot to live and we live to scoot on Long Island." Members ride a wide variety of classic and modern scooters. Contact: hornrts_sc@yahoo.com; www.thehornets.cc/newsite.html

Atlanta's Burning...for Scooters!

Evidence that Atlanta's becoming a hot spot for scootering? The Vespa Club of America staged its annual Amerivespa rally in nearby Madison in 2003. Want more? Stroll into Moto Bravo in the super-trendy Buckhead part of town. Reflecting the general scooter scene, the shop sells and restores old Vespas and Lambrettas, but also deals in brand-new Aprilia, Kymco, Derbi, and Stella scoots.

Jeff Hyatt is a resident mechanic at Moto Bravo, having moved here from southern California. Familiar with the SoCal scooter culture, as well as that up north in San Francisco, Jeff boldly predicts that "Atlanta is going to be the next big boom city. The interest here is phenomenal, for both vintage and new bikes." Besides Buckhead, scooters can be regularly spotted in the Highlands and Decatur.

Not long after he arrived—sans the Series 2 Lambretta he had to sell before the move east—Jeff joined the Imperial Scooter Club. "It's very active," he states. Members meet once a week, usually at Thinking Man Tavern, a British-style pub in Decatur co-owned by local scooterist Hunter Franklin. Among other scooter-friendly hangouts in Atlanta are The Local, Gravity Club, and Moe's & Joe's.

Scootful in Seattle

It's not much of a stretch to declare Seattle the most passionate scooter city in America. It's hard to pinpoint exactly why—it's certainly not 365 days of warm, sunny weather—but scootering has maintained a distinct presence in the Puget Sound area since the 1980s. That's when riders of classic Italian scoots started finding each other, and those vintage devotees remain the core of the city's scooterists. Yet it's a scooter-friendly place, too, so riders of modern machines are generally accepted in clubs, on rides, at rallies and in the dozens of bars and other two-wheeler hangouts.

Perhaps no one knows more about this diverse subculture than Victor Voris, founder and president of the very active Vespa Club of Seattle. "For the past 20 years, Seattle has had a huge scooter community, but its organization has varied over the years," Victor writes on VCOS's website. "At this time, there are about 750 people who own and ride European scooters around Puget Sound. This is probably the largest number of riders the Northwest has ever seen, and there are very few places in North America that can boast such numbers."

The first Scooter Insanity rally still attracts a wild bunch every September to ogle awesome custom scoots and ride en masse. Predictably, scooter clubs thrive in Seattle. Besides VCOS, which meets at 8 p.m. every second Tuesday at the Fairview Bar & Grill, there's the Emerald City Flying Monkeys, R-Gang (sponsors of the annual Meant to Offend rally), the all-girl Belladonnas, Los Gatos (caters to Spanish-speaking riders), the Wussys, and the Northwest Scooter Enthusiasts, which leans toward moderns scooters, especially Japanese models.

Full Moon SC, Syracuse

Members welcome owners of both classic and modern scooters. Contact: danny@dreamscape.com; www.dreamscape.com/danny/fmsc

Negative Image SC, Rochester

Serving Western New Yorkers with an interest in all motor scooters. Contact: spontin@rochester.rr.com; http://autos.groups.yahoo.com/group/NISC

Ohio

Pride of Cleveland SC

"Live near Cleveland? Like spending your summer weekends traveling, meeting interesting people and learning all about the scooter lifestyle?" Contact: pocphil@sbcglobal.net; www.poc.itgo.com

Mid-Ohio Classic Scooters, Columbus

"Dedicated to the preservation and restoration of classic motor scooters. All makes welcome!" Contact: BZengel@aol.com; www.geocities.com/mocs95

Ten Year Lates SC, Cincinnati

XYLs meet at The Comet in Northside every Wednesday at 7:30 p.m. "We don't discriminate—vintage, new, Vespa, Lambretta, motorcycle, moped —whatever you got, come hang out." Contact: casey@sugarburninc.com; www.tenyearlates.com/ver2

Oregon

Twist & Play SC, Portland

Meets every Tuesday night at 9:30 at the Shanghai Tunnel. Contact: info@twistnplay.com; http://twistnplay.doughnut.net

Hell's Belles SC, Portland

All-girls club whose members "like to socialize, ride and participate in fun stuff together. Our club is open to any woman who rides a scooter." Contact: hellsbelles@hellsbelles.org; www.hellsbelles.org

Top Dead Center SC, Eugene

Contact: radiojh@comcast.net

Pennsylvania

Hostile City SC, Philadelphia

Organizes annual 4th of July rally. Contact: ginger@working-class.com; www.hostilecitysc.com

Pittsburgh Vintage SC

"Always welcoming new people to ride in the area!" Contact: ph2c@andrew.cmu.edu; http://go.to/pvsc

Rhode Island

Death or Glory SC, Providence

Organizes Sunday rides and a summer rally. Contact: dogsc@another-face.com; http://dogsc.another-face.com

Texas

Get Bent SC, Dallas

"Laid-back group with mostly older Vespas, but a mix of newer Vespas, Stellas or whatever rolls." Meets to ride every Sunday at 3 p.m. at the Dubliner. Fun website. Contact: scooterboy@getbent-sc.com; www.getbent-sc.com

Scooter Union SC, Houston

"Riders of all different types of scooters from Houston to Clear Lake. We organize rides just about every weekend, from pub crawls through the heart of downtown to all-day rides through the countryside." Contact: webmaster@scooterunion.com // www.scooterunion.com

Utah

Brigham's Bees SC

"Our aim is to provide camaraderie for those who love admiring, restoring and riding Italian scooters." Contact: www.brighamsbees.org

Washington

Vespa Club of Seattle

"Our interests lie primarily with the Vespa and other classic European scooters, but all scooterists are welcome." General meetings are held on the second Tuesday of each month at the Lucky Dog Café. Contact: www.vespaclubofseattle.com

Northwest Scooter Enthusiasts, Seattle

Have been riding around Seattle and Puget Sound on all makes and models of scooters since 1998. Meets the last Wednesday of each month at Latona Pub. Contact: nwse@soundrider.com; www.soundrider.com/nwse

Los Gatos Gordos SC, Seattle

Meets the second Monday of every month at the Honey Hole at around 7:30 p.m. Contact: los_gatos_gordos@hotmail.com; www.losgatosgordos.com

Maxi Scooter Riders Association of Washington, Tacoma

"Does mingling with others who share your common interest in maxi scooters sound appealing? Then come ride with the Northwest's premier touring scooter club." Contact: steve@maxiscooter.org; www.maxiscooter.org

Specialty club

Talk about model-specific: Every year, a group of people who keep old Cushmans alive meet in Nebraska, where the 1950s-era scooters were made.

Scoote

So ou've decided to take the plunge and enter the Scooter Life. You've examined all the models and made your choice. You scoot home, pleased with your purchase, but then as you look at your new ride, you realize—you're not done shopping.

Along with designer-label paint schemes, slick European styling, and the latest in technology, scooters offer their owners the chance to accessorize like nobody's business. On these pages, check out some of the more popular sorts of gear, add-ons, and just plain stuff that you can add to your scooter or scooter lifestyle. Most manu-facturers offer accessories that work with their bikes only, but there are some items that work across models and makes. Shop around, in person and online, to find what you need.

Bug-free ride
The windshield or windscreen is a popular add-on. They attach to the handlebars.

Stuff

Rack 'em up
Carrying stuff is always a consideration when choosing a scooter. Look for racks that fit your needs and lifestyle.

Chrome, baby!
Racks of all sorts are available in that shiny stuff that turns heads and creates work with the polishing rag: Chrome kits are key for keeping your bike shiny.

Stylish in leather

Leather saddlebags can not only carry your stuff, but look extremely chic, too.

Spare tire stylin'

You can attach a spare tire to most scooters for emergency use. Nice-looking cases like this one make precaution prettier.

Hook up

This Vespa includes a luggage hook in the seat perfect for holding this branded bag, designed to fit inside the leg hole area.

Super storage

Again, carrying space is at a premium and creative uses of space like this can be found, too.

Larger scooter models have room under the seat for storage. This Vespa is designed to hold two helmets snugly in the locking underseat compartment.

A touch of tech

Who needs keys when you can pop open the locking seat with this remote control device?

Ultramodern touch

Some models come with a charger plug-in under the seat, perfect for keeping your cell phone hot.

Protection up top

Not only are helmets a good idea, but in most cases, they are the law. There are many styles, and as the saying goes, protect your head like it's the only one you'll get.

Scooter Glossary

Ride the ride, talk the talk: Here's a handy guide to key words and phrases from the world of scootering:

Classic scooters

Metal-body scooters made before the 1980s, usually Vespas and Lambrettas, whose distinct Italian styling has endured and been copied since they first appeared in the mid-1940s. Also called "vintage scooters."

Four-stroke engine

Internal combustion engine that burns gas and oil separately, thereby generating less pollution than two-stroke engines.

Lambretta

The "other" classic Italian scooter, introduced in 1947 by Innocenti. Lambretta and Vespa were worldwide rivals until Innocenti sold its operations in 1972.

Maxi scooters

Modern scooters with engines generally larger than 200cc (some up to 650cc), designed for high-speed, long-distance travel. Also called "touring scooters."

Mods

Short for "moderns," a subculture of British teenagers in the 1960s who wore jackets and ties and hooded parkas, listened to soul music and rode scooters. Their bitter feuds with rival "Rockers"—who wore black leather, listened to rock and roll and rode motorcycles—were dramatized in the 1979 movie *Quadrophenia*.

Modern scooters

General term for bikes introduced in the 1980s, featuring sleek, modernistic styling similar to European motorcycles. Body parts often made of plastic and/or fiberglass. Also called "sport scooters."

Moped

Legally speaking, motorized two-wheeled vehicles with step-through frames, engine sizes of 50cc or less, and that don't exceed 30 mph are classified as mopeds in most U.S. states. Bikes with larger, faster engines are considered motorcycles. Generally, mopeds also feature bicycle-like pedals.

Rally

An organized event for scooterists, featuring judging of scooters, rides, and parties.

Retro scooters

Current lookalikes of classic scooters produced and marketed by a wide variety of international companies. "Retro" describes a design style evoking products of the past.

Two-stroke engine

Internal combustion engine that burns gas and oil together, generally resulting in greater lower-end torque and better fuel efficiency than a four-stroke engine. Older two-strokes, however, emit high levels of pollution.

Twist-and-go

Scooters equipped with automatic transmissions that require no clutch or shifting. Also called "twist and ride" and "automatic" scooters. (Also the name of a scooter brand.)

Vespa

The prototypical, classic Italian—and best-known—scooter, first introduced in 1946 by parent company Piaggio. The company continues to produce new models based on their original designs (as well as the Piaggio line of modern scooters).

Scooter Web Sites

scootrs.com/index.cfm
Along with being a resource for parts and maintenance tips, great clearinghouse for scoot news from around the world

scooterbbs.com
Great bulletin boards

www.piaggiousa.com
Piaggio scooters (Vespa has a separate site, but you can get there from here)

lambretta.org
Lambretta Club USA site

www.scootertune.com/link/link3.htm
Exhaustive list of links to manufacturers worldwide

www.scootering.com
"UK's No.1 Scootering Magazine"

ScooterHelp.com
Best place to go online for mechanical help from peers

www.genuinescooters.com
All about Stella (will take you to Scooterworks, home of lots of Vespa and Lambretta parts)

www.scootquarterly.com
Scoot! Quarterly magazine

www.nh-scooters.com/article/frontpage/1
Scoot Free or Die, club in New Hampshire, has great stuff

gsx.suzuki.com/~sucycles/sr_03/scooter/fs_an650.htm

www.cycleimports.com
Official site for Derbi (part of the Piaggio group)

www.twistngo.com
Another UK scoot 'zine

www.quadrophenia.net
More than you'd ever want about the movie

www.hobbytech.com
Good site for Cushman history, pix, etc.

www.lcgb.co.uk/index.html
Lambretta Club of UK, loaded with goodies

www.yamaha-motor.com/products/models.asp?lid=2&lc=mcy&cid=8
Home site of Yamaha Motor Corp.

www.nycscooterist.com
If you're scootin' in the Big Apple, bite here

scooterworks.com
Online catalog for vintage parts, accessories, etc.

www.scootermaniac.org
From this French-language home page, click on the English language button
(the American flag) to check out an incredible repository of historical photos and
information on scooters

vespa.org/
Vespa Club of San Francisco, with great links area

www.lambretta.it
Italian site

www.vespafascination.com

www.dreamscape.com/danny/scootclubs/index2.html
Good list of clubs, though some out of date

www.scooterworldmag.com/index.html
A fledgling Denver-based 'zine, though may be closely affiliated with city's Sportique
Scooters retailer

www.2strokebuzz.com
"Kicking Ass and Leaking Gas"; fun site based in Chicago

www.vespaclubusa.org/index2.htm
Vespa Club of America. "The Vespa Club of America (VCOA) is a non-profit organization
dedicated to collecting, restoring and preserving European motorscooters."

Index

A

Accessories 114-119
Alley, Kirstie 49
Ameican Scooter Racing Association 108
Andress, Ursula 40
Atlanta 106, 109
Auto-Fauteuil 13, 38
Autoglider 14, 38
Autoped 13

B

Bagley, Ron 97
Barbie, Vespa 48
Brack, Kenny 51
Bullock, Sandra 8
Buying a scooter 50-61

C

Cappadona, Tony 96
Celebrities on scooters 34, 36, 38-40, 44-45, 48-49
Chaplin, Charlie 40
Chicago 16, 60, 66, 106
China 7, 9, 22
Clubs (listing by state) 103-111
Clooney, George 48
Cushman scooters 7, 15, 16, 19, 26, 36, 47, 52, 62, 111

D

Dallas 37, 97, 111
D'Ascanio, Corradino 26

E

Eastern Scooter Racing Association 108
Early scooters 7, 12-21
Elleham (Denmark) 13
Elmore, Austin 16

F

Fashion connections 9, 24, 45, 46
France 9, 15, 17, 19, 22, 35, 108

G

Gauthier, Georges 13
Geisenhof, Hans 12
Great Britain 7-8, 17, 22, 35-36, 42, 105

H

Helmets 11, 56, 82, 117, 119
Hepburn, Audrey 7, 37, 38
Heston, Charlton 40
Hildebrand & Wolfmuller 12-13
Hoffman Werke 35
Holden, William 40
Honda 7, 8, 10, 19, 22, 37, 54, 60, 62, 63, 73, 80, 86, 107
Hyatt, Jeff 109

I

India 7, 9, 22, 35, 65, 66, 101, 107
Innocenti 12, 18, 24, 27, 29, 31, 34, 35, 36, 37, 108
Innocenti, Fernando 29
International scooter types 18-19, 21, 34-35, 54, 98-101
Isles de Saints 90
Italy travel 100

J

Jedi Knights 102, 106-107

K

Key West 90, 96, 106

L

Lambretta 6-8, 12, 14, 17-19, 21, 22, 24-25, 29-32, 34, 37, 39-40, 42, 44, 62, 68
Lambretta Club USA 102, 105
Las Vegas 6, 43, 108
Law, Jude 44
Laws 7, 10-11, 37, 56, 94, 119
Leno, Jay 8, 58
Lollobrigida, Gina 40
London scooters 101
Los Corazones Negros 107
Luggage 48, 86, 88, 116, 117

M

Maguire, Tobey 44
Maintenance 52-53, 84-89
Malaguti USA 97
Mansfield, Jayne 40
Manufacturers, list of 60

Martin, Joel 97
Martin, Steve 43
McCaleb, Philip 107
Miami 21 ,37, 43, 60, 96-97, 106-106
Mid-America Scooter Sports 108
Mods 8, 14, 40, 44
Motorcycle Safety Foundation 58, 94

N
Ner-a-car 15
Nerachar, Carl 15
Newman, Paul 40, 42
New York City scooters 36-37, 94-95

O
Ogilvy, Jonathan 92

P
Paltrow, Gwyneth 50
Paris 38, 101
Peck, Gregory 7, 37, 38
Piaggio 10, 12, 17, 18, 22, 24-26, 31, 32, 34,
    37, 60, 63-66, 69, 76, 81, 83, 97, 107-108
    (see also Vespa)
(also see Vespa)
Piaggio, Enrico 16, 17, 25, 29, 34, 36
Piaggio, Rinaldo 17, 25
Pink Panther 42-43

Q
Quadrophenia 8, 41-42

R
Rapini, Luis 97
Rizzuto, Phil "Scooter" 10
Rockers 8, 40
Rogers, Josh 47
Roman Holiday 7, 38, 42

S
Salsbury 15, 19, 36, 39
Salsbury, E. Foster 16
San Francisco 92-93
Schaefer, Chad 107
Schieffelin, Wen and Zach 94
Scoot Quarterly 3, 46, 66, 102
Scooter Girl 44
Scooter racing 9, 95, 108
Scooterworks USA 107
Seattle 37, 110-111
Sellers, Peter 42

Steinbeck, John 39
Sting 8, 49
Suzuki 10, 21, 22, 60, 63, 82

T
Torre, Pier Luigi 29

U
Unibus 14, 38

V
Vespa
    Celebrity owners 34, 36, 49
    Competition with Lambretta 26-36
    Created 6, 12, 24-25
    ET series 48, 55, 64, 83, 97
    First prototype 26
    Granturismo 37
    In ads 30, 36
    In movies 27, 49
    International licenses 35
    In the U.S. 20-21, 22, 36, 44
    PX Series 66, 107
    Use by Mods 14
Vespa Club of America 102, 106
Vietnam 98

W
Wacker, Watts 48
Wayne, John 34, 39-40
Weindorf, Bob 58, 84
Welbike 16-17
Welch, Raquel 40
Whitney, April 47
Who, The 8
Wolfmuller, Alois 12
Wood, Natalie 40

Y
Yamaha 10, 19, 21, 22, 54, 60, 71, 79, 83, 107

Z
Zorn, Mike 47

Photo and Illustration Credits

The producers and the publisher would like to thank the many scooter manufacturers who were so generous with their assistance in providing the many photos of scooters, modern and "classic," that appear in this book, especially Piaggio USA, makers of the Vespa. Other companies that provided photos and help include Malaguti, Derbi, Kymko, Lambretta, Bajaj, and Honda.

Cover photos: Hepburn/Peck, Mr. Piaggio, Clooney by Bettmann/Corbis; old air check, Quadrophenia scene by Hulton Archive; racers, old and new Vespas by Piaggio USA.

Interior photos:
(t = top; b = bottom; c = center; r = right; l = left)
Agence FrancePress/Corbis: 48t
AP/Wide World: 10b, 36, 39, 49t, 51, 52, 57, 87, 97, 103, 104, 111
Morton Beebe/Corbis: 2-3
Bettmann/Corbis: 17, 21, 25, 38b, 42(3); 53
Ralph Clevenger: 48

Curbishley-Baird/The Kobal Collection: 20t, 41
Mike Eliason: 85b, 86b, 88, 117t
Getty Images: 6t, 7tr, 10t, 58, 93, 120
Hulton Archive: 8b, 13, 14, 15t, 16b, 19, 29, 33, **40, 84**
Kelly-Mooney/Corbis: 91
Arnaldo Magnani/Getty Images: 44b
John and Lisa Merrill/Corbis: 99
Peggy Storm/Getty Images: 44t
Alberto Pellaschiar/AFP/Corbis: 54
ReutersNewMedia/Corbis: 45t
Vittoriano Rastelli/Corbis: 98
ScooterManiac.org: 12tb, 20b
Peter Turnley/Corbis: 101
Matt Smith/Getty Images: 50
SwimInk/Corbis: 38t;
Patrick Ward/Corbis: 90
WireImage: 5c, 49b

Acknowledgments

When Shoreline Publishing Group honcho Jim Buckley called me about writing a book on scooters, it sounded pretty straightforward: trace the histories of Vespa, Lambretta, and a few other big names; report on the resurgence in scootering; describe different types of scooters; provide buying and maintenance tips; identify scoot-friendly cities and clubs.

Boy, was I in for a surprisingly wild ride!

I've been a two-wheeler since age 16, mostly on motorcycles, but have long appreciated the simpler pleasures of scootering. However, not until I ran smack into the headwind of the scooter subculture with this book did I realize the fantastic international story behind these incredible machines and the people who ride them.

I became much more acquainted with both in the course of this project. For their kind help and sharp insights, I need to thank several, including Doug Day at Scooter Centrale in Plainville, CT; Victor Voris, founder of the Vespa Club of Seattle and Big People Scooters; Josh Rogers, editor of Scoot! Quarterly; Adam Baker of Sportique Scooters in Denver; Kimberlee Auletta and Costantino Sambuy of Piaggio/Vespa USA; Joel Martin of Malaguti USA; Al Kolvites of Bajaj USA; Philip McCaleb of Scooterworks; and the dozens of other individuals at scooter companies, shops and clubs who generously shared their time to talk scoots. [Shoreline would like to add our thanks to Bob Weindorf of Vespa Santa Barbara.]

Mr. Buckley's guidance and patience were greatly appreciated, as was my wife Sue's indulgence in listening to months of scooter rants (you, too, kids). Mostly, though, I'd like to thank the dedicated and ever-growing legions of scooterists—of both the vintage and modern variety—who have provided the rubber-meets-the-road inspiration for this very fun effort. Keep your shiny side up! Bob Woods, Madison, CT, February 2004

About the Author

Bob Woods is a veteran magazine writer who has contributed to *Sports Illustrated*, *Newsweek International*, and *Money*, as well as several Web sites. A lifelong motorcycle rider (and owner of a still-running 23-year-old Suzuki), he was the editor of *Harley-Davidson: The Official 100th Anniversary Magazine*. He has also written books on baseball, extreme sports, and auto racing for young readers. He lives in Madison, Connecticut (and has his eye on a sweet little Vespa PX).